STATE
TAXATION
AND
ECONOMIC
DEVELOPMENT

The Council of State Planning Agencies is a membership organization comprised of the planning and policy staff of the nation's governors. Through its Washington office, the Council provides assistance to individual states on a wide spectrum of policy matters. The Council also performs policy and technical research on both state and national issues. The Council was formed in 1966; it became affiliated with The National Governors' Association in 1975.

In addition to *Studies in State Development Policy,* the Council publishes:

■ *CSPA Working Papers.* Current volumes address: environmental protection and economic development; commercial bank financing for small business enterprise; venture capital and urban development; the impact of regional shopping malls; the operation of minority capital markets; and the public service costs of alternative development patterns. A full list of current volumes is available on request.
■ *State Planning Issues.* A journal concerning the problems and practice of planning in the states. Published twice yearly.
■ *The State Planning Series.* Sixteen short papers dealing with financial management, citizen participation, econometrics, urban and rural development, policy development techniques, multi-state organizations, federal-state partnerships, and other issues of concern to state officials.

See page 159 to order *Studies in State Economic Development.*

The Council of State Planning Agencies
Hall of the States
444 North Capitol Street
Washington, D.C. 20001
(202) 624-5386

Robert N. Wise
Director

Michael Barker
Associate Director for
Community and Economic Development

STATE TAXATION AND ECONOMIC DEVELOPMENT

ROGER J. VAUGHAN

COVER: *"Map 1963," by Jasper Johns. Collection Albert Saalsfield. Grateful acknowledgement is made to Mr. Johns for allowing the reproduction of his work.*

Partial funding support for this volume was received from the Office of Economic Research, Economic Development Administration, the U.S. Department of Commerce. The views and findings it contains are the author's, and do not necessarily represent those of the Economic Development Administration or the members or staff of The Council of State Planning Agencies. Reproduction of any part of this volume is permitted for any purpose of the United States Government.

Library of Congress Catalog Number: 79-54265

ISBN: 0-934842-00-0

Printed in the United States of America. First printing - 1979.

Format conceptualization and series coordination: Katherine Kinsella
Design: Kathy Jungjohann
Typesetting and Layout: Teri Grimwood
Printing and binding services: George Banta Co.

To tax and to please,
No more than to love and be wise,
Is not given to men.

Edmund Burke, 1774

ACKNOWLEDGEMENTS

The preparation of this paper has benefited from advice and assistance from many sources. Michael Barker of the Council of State Planning Agencies has provided suggestions and a steady flow of references and data. Helpful comments have been received from Michael Kieschnick of Harvard University, Stephen Gold of the Urban Institute, Jonathan Rowe of the Multistate Tax Commission, Sandra Kanter of MIT, and Diane Fuchs of Rosapepe, Fuchs and Associates. The paper has also relied on the data and discussions of issues in the numerous source documents cited in the bibliography. The research of the Advisory Commission on Intergovernmental Relations has proved particularly useful.

Errors of fact and interpretation remain the sole responsibility of the author.

TABLE OF CONTENTS

TABLES

PREFACE

This paper analyzes the role of state taxation policies in shaping state economic development. It is one of a series of papers addressing state economic development issues prepared for the Council of State Planning Agencies under a contract from the U.S. Economic Development Administration.

The purpose of these papers is to provide information and analysis for those policy makers at the state and local levels charged with responsibility for economic development and fiscal affairs. This paper is organized to address the following questions:

■ What's wrong with—and how can we improve—the present state/local fiscal structure?
■ What can states do to improve the efficiency and equity of business taxes and business tax incentives?
■ What can states do to improve personal taxes?
■ How can states best respond to the fiscal limitation movement?

Although the focus is on *state* taxes, their influence can only be understood within the context of the whole intergovernmental tax structure. Therefore, this paper also analyzes ways in which federal and local tax policy could be improved.

No new empirical research was undertaken for this study. Rather, the results of many studies are synthesized to present an overview of the complex interactions between taxes and development and to evaluate present fiscal policies.

The object is not to make specific and detailed policy recommendations, since these usually depend on the specifics of the local fiscal structure, but rather to suggest the advantages and disadvantages of alternative fiscal policies.

SUMMARY
AND RECOMMENDATIONS

State tax policy is in disarray: states compete for footloose firms by offering expensive tax holidays; households are in revolt against rising property tax burdens; cities demand state aid for social services; and the federal government mandates costly programs that must be paid for with state funds. By-passed by the federal grant programs spawned by the recent recession, state officials have been trapped in a reactive role and have been left out of the urban policy debate. The present state tax structure reflects the hasty application of band-aids rather than the considered surgery that is necessary to meet current economic problems.

This paper examined how the structure of state and local taxes can best be adapted to meet these problems. It approached the problem from a broad perspective, analyzing not only business taxes, but also the state/local fiscal structure and personal taxes, since these issues also influence the local pattern of development. The paper's conclusions, summarized below, should help local policy makers in the difficult tasks that confront them.

WHAT SHOULD A STATE ECONOMIC DEVELOPMENT STRATEGY LOOK LIKE?

Taxes are only one factor among many—and a relatively minor one—that affect state economic development. The quality of the local labor force, transportation facilities, energy prices, and population growth all contribute to shaping local development. In fact, population growth may be the single most important factor. Households are not only drawn by local job openings but also by an attractive residential and recreational environment. This implies that:

An economic development strategy must aim at attracting skilled workers as well as factories. Concentrating on industrial parks and business tax incentives at the expense of residential amenities will meet with only limited success.

As the distribution of jobs and people change in response to technological change and other market forces, as well as to public sector policies, underlying market conditions change. Wages and land prices are driven up in growth areas, while costs fall in slower growing *3* regions. The future is not an indefinite extension of the past. A loss of manufacturing jobs may be counterbalanced by an increase in service industry employment. The lesson is that:

An economic development strategy must recognize changing local comparative advantage, and not attempt to wind the clock back. For the Northeast, and for many urban areas, manufacturing can no longer be the main engine of growth.

Most local employment growth occurs through the birth of new firms and the expansion of existing, small companies. Very little growth (or decline) results from the inmigration (or outmigration) of firms. Taxes play only a minor role in the location decisions of migrating companies. Therefore:

An economic development strategy must focus on the overall economic climate, and not waste resources on special incentives for a few favored firms. It must encompass a broad range of policies, including training programs, infrastructure development, and capital mobility as well as a balanced tax structure.

Finally, the relatively small role played by taxes does not imply that state governments are powerless to influence growth and development. Positive and coordinated leadership and a minimum of red tape are important considerations.

WHAT GUIDELINES SHOULD A STATE EMPLOY TO IMPROVE ITS TAX STRUCTURE?

The primary purpose of taxes is to raise revenues to pay for local services. This must be achieved with as little disruption as possible to businesses and households, as fairly as possible, and at the lowest possible administrative cost. The following guidelines should help in the formulation of local fiscal policy.

Efficiency
■ The overall burden of taxes should reflect the local preference for public services.
■ The tax structure should not encourage undesirable reactions by taxpayers, such as business or household relocation.

Equity
■ The greater a taxpayer's resources, the greater his tax payments should be.
■ Taxpayers with similar resources should incur similar tax burdens, all other things being equal.

4

■ The tax burden for taxpayers with similar resources should be related to the value of public services received.

Administrative Cost
■ The tax should be simple to collect and to enforce.
■ The tax revenue should be predictable.
■ The tax revenue should grow over time as the demand for public services grows.
■ The tax revenue should be cyclically stabilizing.

These guidelines cannot be rigidly enforced, since they are not necessarily compatible. An increase in efficiency may only be achieved at a loss of equity, for example. But the guidelines do allow these trade-offs to be made explicitly as fiscal policy is debated.

There are also constraints on the extent to which state policy makers can pursue these goals. First, they must operate within the overall structure of fiscal federalism, in which they are limited by the actions of the federal and local governments. Second, states are limited by their desire to maintain sound bond ratings. And finally, they are limited by the fact that there is a great deal that is not known about who pays for specific taxes and how taxes affect business and household behavior.

WHAT SHOULD STATES DO ABOUT THE STATE/LOCAL FISCAL STRUCTURE?

The allocation of responsibility for revenue collection and service delivery between states and local governments has been seriously strained by recent developments. First, state governments are doing too little to equalize fiscal capacity among their component jurisdictions—a fact recognized in a number of recent court decisions concerning school finance and by the federal government in its recent grant programs. Second, the profusion of federal grants that enabled many fiscally troubled cities to survive the mid-1970s recession more-or-less intact are likely to dry up. States will be expected to step into the gap. Third, the property tax, the main source of local government revenue, has become the target of the taxpayers' revolt. It is increasingly difficult for high taxing jurisdictions to raise revenues.

There are several steps that states can take to improve the state/local fiscal structure:

■ *Encourage metropolitan-wide tax base sharing.* Uniting poor central cities with their relatively affluent suburbs can provide much needed fiscal relief. Although this is a politically difficult step, states can provide some incentives by rewarding tax sharing areas with

5

higher grants—a policy that the federal government should follow.

■ *Retarget state revenue sharing grants.* At present, most state aid is distributed on the basis of population, which minimizes its redistributive impact. Aid can be better targeted to needy areas.

■ *Introduce or expand state-financed circuit breakers.* These are an effective way to provide relief to low-income households. To be as equitable as possible, these should be extended to renters and place an upper income limit on eligibility. Federal assistance should be provided, perhaps using the state portion of General Revenue Sharing.

■ *The progressivity of state taxes should be increased in those states with regressive systems.* This can be done either by switching from regressive to progressive taxes or increasing the progressivity of present taxes. However, a sudden and sharp increase in progressivity may encourage the outmigration of high-income households.

■ *States should continue to lobby for increased federal aid for programs targeted to the poor.*

WHAT SHOULD STATES DO ABOUT BUSINESS TAXES?

There is a popular myth that a reduction in the level of state business taxes will produce a flood of new development. The truth is very different. The level of business taxes has very little impact on the local growth rate or on the interstate location decisions of firms. To some extent, intrastate differences in business taxes contribute to the movement of firms away from high-taxing central cities to less heavily taxed suburbs and non-metropolitan areas. Payroll taxes exacerbate the problem of unemployment, particularly among the less-skilled. Investment may be deterred by high local taxes. Some policies which may improve the efficiency and equity of the present business tax structure include:

■ *States should resist the temptation to cut business taxes in order to stimulate development.* Reduced business taxes have little effect on location or investment decisions. While states should ensure that their taxes are not greatly out of line with those of their neighbors, a stronger case can be made for reducing personal taxes to encourage development by attracting skilled workers than for business tax cutting.

■ *States should take steps to reduce interjurisdictional differences in tax rates.* The relevant steps are described above.

■ *States should review their allocation formulas for firms operating in more than one state.* Several states have formed a tax compact to ensure that multi-state companies pay taxes on their full tax base. While other states should follow suit, this will necessitate a simplification of interstate tax legislation and a move toward a more standardized definition of tax base. Federal legislation will be necessary for this.

■ *Some states should consider using a tax on value added to replace their business taxes.* The Value Added Tax produces more stable revenue, is simpler to administer, and does not discourage investment as much as traditional business income taxes.

■ *States should consider encouraging their jurisdictions to shift some of the burden of the property tax away from improvements and onto land.* This would reduce the deterrent to new investment inherent in the property tax, and discourage speculative land holding (which delays urban redevelopment and creates sprawl). The administrative difficulties in such a shift are severe, but not insuperable.

WHAT SHOULD STATES DO ABOUT TAX INCENTIVES?

States have devoted considerable manpower and resources to devising tax breaks for firms that move in, firms that threaten to move out, and firms that promise to expand. There is little evidence that these costly programs have had much influence on either investment or location decisions. These misplaced energies and mortgaged tax receipts should be redirected in several ways:

■ *With federal assistance, states should reduce the special incentive programs they offer.* The federal government could penalize states that offer such incentives through provisions in grant allocation formulas. States should concern themselves with the overall economic climate, not on bribing a few footloose firms.

■ *States should act to reduce interjurisdictional incentive tax competition.* This can be done by reducing fiscal disparities, through legal prohibition, or through grant allocation policy.

■ *The exemption of the interest from industrial development bonds— and from state and municipal bonds—from federal and state income taxes should be replaced with an interest rate subsidy.*

■ *If states are to use tax incentives, they should be in the form of wage subsidies.* Wage subsidies reduce the cost of labor to employers and can be targeted to the hard-to-employ. They should be in the form of tax credits against payroll taxes to be most effective. A wage subsidy is one of the few policies that would effectively *create* jobs.

■ *States should rely more heavily on infrastructure development and the reduction of red tape as inducements to industry, and less on tax manipulation.*

WHAT SHOULD STATES DO ABOUT PERSONAL TAXES?

The present burden of personal taxes collected by state and local governments is inefficient and inequitable. It is *inefficient* inasmuch as high state income tax rates tend to reduce the net inmigration of high income households,

7

leaving a heavier burden on the less affluent who remain. High taxes are also capitalized in high wages, discouraging local economic growth. High central city property taxes—used to finance extensive redistributive services—have encouraged the more affluent to move to more homogeneous suburban jurisdictions. High property taxes also tend to depress property values and discourage investment. The system is *inequitable* because the income tax in several states is regressive. Such income tax provisions as incentives for homeownership and standard deductions are also highly regressive. In addition, the property tax is regressive, and its inequity is compounded by poor administration. States have several options to improve the efficiency and equity of personal taxes:

■ *Income Tax.* Standard deductions can be replaced by standard tax credits. Tax incentives for homeownership can be reduced, or mitigated by allowances for renters. The levels of tax credits and tax brackets can be indexed to the local cost of living, so that inflation does not provide governments with a "fiscal bonus." The deduction of state and local taxes from federal taxable income should be disallowed and replaced with extended federal revenue sharing. The tax structure should be simplified and standardized among states.

■ *Property Taxes.* The efficiency of assessment should be greatly increased. State-financed circuit breakers and shifting some of the burden onto land would improve equity and efficiency.

■ *Sales Tax.* Exemptions for food and medicine should be used in all states to improve equity. Some consideration should be given to extending the tax to cover professional services.

■ *Fees and Charges.* Fees and charges offer an efficient and equitable way for states and localities to raise revenue and ensure effective use of public services, especially where there are prevailing tax limitations. They are especially effective in covering the costs of new development or redevelopment (sewering, water hook-ups, etc.).

INTRODUCTION

The 1970s have been anything but kind to state governments. Major metropolitan areas, traditionally both engines of growth and major sources of tax revenues, have lost jobs and veered toward fiscal insolvency. Mayors and federal officials have blamed states for not caring. Social programs, grown as a result of local political pressures and federal mandate, have inflated expenditures. Swollen federal grant programs have by-passed states and gone directly to local jurisdictions. The rise of the "New South" at the expense of the "Old North" has pitted Sunbelt states against Snowbelt states. The national economy, apparently recession-proof during the 1960s, has faltered, straining unemployment insurance funds, swelling welfare rolls, and leading the jobless to demand aggressive state economic development programs. Taxpayers, whose rising incomes and property values provided localities with annual fiscal dividends, have finally rebelled.

State governments have, for the most part, fallen into a reactive role. Their functions have proliferated, often unwillingly. They are forced to work through a bewildering number of regional organizations and special districts. Federal red tape has multiplied. States must compete with cities for federal funds.

These changes necessitate a rethinking of the role of the states within our intergovernmental system. This paper examines a part of this complex puzzle—how can the state/local tax structure be modified in order to be an effective economic development tool? In the past, state involvement in economic development has been principally concentrated on physical development. After nearly a year of monitoring state community assistance programs, the Advisory Commission on Intergovernmental Relations concluded that: "Although broadly based structural and fiscal reforms have been widely endorsed as mechanisms by which states might ameliorate local development patterns, the adoption of such reforms has been relatively limited (*Information Bulletin*, January 1979)." To encourage a more radical approach, we must ask a number of very basic questions. How do state business and personal taxes influence state economic development? What will the impact of the fiscal limitation movement be? How do federal programs and policies affect state fiscal actions? How can the structure of state taxes be changed to improve efficiency and equity?

The following chapter defines overall state economic development goals, both in responding to local development problems and in the way they interact, or conflict, with federal and local goals. Chapter **9**

2 outlines the factors that influence the process of economic growth. This allows us to place in perspective the role played by taxes, and to identify the direct and indirect links between tax policy and growth. Chapter 3 sets out the guidelines to apply when developing state tax systems—efficiency, equity, and administrative ease. It also outlines existing constraints on state fiscal policy, including the fiscal federal structure, the degree of fiscal strain in different states, and our lack of knowledge concerning tax incidence and impacts.

Chapter 4 discusses the problems inherent in the present state/local fiscal structure, including inequity, the dwindling availability of federal funds, and the problems associated with reliance on the property tax at the local level. Alternative ways to improve the structure are outlined.

Chapters 5 and 6 analyze the effectiveness, equity, and administrative ease of business taxes and special business tax incentives. They also suggest ways in which present policies could be improved. The discussion encompasses the effects of inter- and intrastate differences on the overall tax level, the effectiveness of targeted fiscal incentives on business, and alternatives to the corporate income tax and the local property tax. The examination of personal taxes in Chapter 7 describes how property and income taxes affect household migration and property investment and outlines ways to improve the present system. The origins and impact of the fiscal limitation movement are described in Chapter 8, together with some recommendations on how the states may avoid its more disruptive consequences. An annotated bibliography is provided at the end of this report; it will allow those interested to pursue the topics covered in more detail.

1
WHAT IS ECONOMIC DEVELOPMENT POLICY?

Economic development remains remarkably difficult to define positively. Specialists debate target rates of growth and unemployment, and unacceptable rates of inflation, but leave the central definition nebulous. In fact, this omission is understandable, at least from the viewpoint of public policy analysis. *Economic development policy, at all levels of government, is best understood as the response to perceived problems, not as an attempt to meet targets.*

The effectiveness of state and local development policies must be judged on the basis of their ability to redress those problems they have been developed to resolve. Tax policies are but one set of weapons in the armory of state economic development policy.

ECONOMIC DEVELOPMENT PROBLEMS

Economic development involves structural change in response to both market forces—technological change, rising incomes, changing international and national growth patterns—and changes in federal, state and local policies. This adaptation is not without cost, nor is it borne equally by all geographic areas, firms, or population groups.

The costs of adjustment include the redevelopment of existing public and private capital, building new facilities, relocating firms and households, and acquiring new skills. These adjustments are not made instantly because employers and employees make decisions with imperfect knowledge about what opportunities are available now and what will happen in the future. Responsibility does not rest solely with workers—to move and to learn new skills—nor with firms—to incorporate new techniques and build new facilities—nor with local governments—to provide new services and adjust local taxes. Adjustment encompasses all these factors. The symptoms of imperfect adjustment are familiar: high local unemployment; the outmigration of firms and households; vacant buildings; low labor force participation rates; and declining income. Faced with these symptoms, the state government may respond in one of three ways: take no action, provide relief or compensation to those affected, or implement a corrective strategy. How it responds depends on its diagnosis of the causes of the problem. Inaction is appropriate if the problem is either not serious or better dealt with at the federal or local level. Relief, in the form of income transfers or municipal grants, is appropriate where the **11** problem is temporary (a cyclical downturn), or is not susceptible to state policy action. A corrective strategy should be undertaken when public policies can effectively address a problem that will not rapidly disappear of its own accord. The focus of this paper is on the last type of response, and in particular, on how tax policies can address local development problems.

In designing a corrective strategy, the state must identify the causes of the economic problem. Why is the local unemployment rate so high? From the state's viewpoint, three classes of problems can be identified:

■ **Places.** Local unemployment may be high because the area has lost its comparative advantage as a place to do business—its infrastructure may be obsolete, or its work force may be concentrated in declining industries.

■ **People.** High unemployment may also reflect the characteristics of the local labor force. The young, ill-educated, or unskilled may experience high unemployment rates.

■ **Jurisdictions.**[1] A local jurisdiction may be unable to provide the population or services necessary for development. High local taxes resulting from a dependent local population, or a small per capita tax base, may slow growth.

Of course, these classes of problems are neither exhaustive nor exclusive. While all areas suffer some degree of economic distress for all of these reasons, the relative severity of distress differs among areas. A steel town in Ohio suffers primarily from a problem of place—its infrastructure is not suitable for modern steel production. High unemployment in the South Bronx may be caused by a lack of training for its residents, while Cleveland's fiscal problems are a jurisdictional problem. Nor are these reasons independent. A concentration of the hard-to-employ in a neighborhood will strain local government resources.

These classes of problems require different types of state policy response. Place problems are normally tackled by state public works projects—new industrial parks, expanded transportation links, and renovated buildings. People problems are addressed through training, work experience programs, and subsidized jobs. Jurisdictional problems have led to expanded grants to local areas and state assumption of local expenditures. Tax policies are part of each type of strategy: tax incentives are offered to firms moving into industrial parks; tax breaks are given to private firms training their workers; and tax sharing is used to help local jurisdictions. The goals of state tax policy are, therefore, interwoven with the more general goals of state economic development policy.

STATE ECONOMIC DEVELOPMENT GOALS

A state's economic development goals are to avoid, or at least lessen, local economic development problems. However, the achievement of these goals is complicated by the imprecise allocation of both fiscal and administrative responsibilities among federal, state and local governments in the "layer cake" structure of fiscal federalism. This section discusses state development goals and the ways in which they may conflict with national and local goals.

National Goals

In addition to pursuing their own goals, states are called upon—sometimes even compelled—to assist the federal government in meeting national objectives. Under the Federal Highway Act, states were called upon to contribute to the construction of a national highway network. States have also been nudged into improving income distribution, administering employment and training programs, abating pollution and enforcing equal rights legislation. Recently, they have been asked to help the Carter Administration in its fight against inflation. What can a state be reasonably expected to do to further national economic goals? How do national goals conflict with state goals?

The following considerations should guide state policy makers in attempting to comply with Washington's wishes:

National Goal	*State Actions*
Stable Prices	There is little, if anything, that states can do to stabilize the rate of inflation. Reducing sales taxes during a period of inflation would have the *cosmetic* effect of reducing the rate of price increases during the month in which the cut was effected. However, prices would continue to rise during the ensuing months as reduced retail prices led to a greater demand for goods and services.
Income Redistribution	States can assist a little in redistributing resources from the affluent to the poor with direct cash transfers and the provision of special services—education, training, health, and housing. States are limited in what they can do about interstate differences in income. (If poor states could export some of their tax burden and rich states import some of theirs,

13

then some shifting of the tax burden could be achieved.)[2] However, intrastate income distribution can be influenced by:

■ the progressivity of the state tax structure;
■ interjurisdictional revenue sharing;
■ state financing of property tax circuit breakers; and
■ state assumption of the cost of services for the poor.

Economic Stabilization   States can participate, in a moderate way, in an effort to reduce economic fluctuations. This is especially useful in view of the fact that states vary considerably in their timing and response to national economic cycles, which makes national expansionary or restrictive policies often inappropriate to state needs. Although states, with two exceptions, are legally prevented from deficit spending during recessions, they can accumulate surpluses during periods of rapid expansion, cutting down consumer demand, and reduce surpluses during recessions.[3] This can lead to some countercyclical impact. Other stabilizing policies by state governments include:

■ adoption of a progressive tax structure;
■ increasing expenditures on automatic stabilizers such as unemployment insurance payments and premiums; and welfare benefits; and
■ tying capital project expenditures to prevailing local economic conditions—delaying construction during booms and expanding activity during recessions. (States do face political pressure to spend surpluses which limit this role.)

Overall, with the exception of income redistribution, the ability of
14 state economic policy to assist in the achievement of national macro-

economic goals is limited.

State Goals

The most obvious purpose of state taxation is to raise revenue to cover state expenditures. However, other criteria are also considered in the process of deciding the structure and level of state taxes, and a state's policy toward local governments.

State Goal	State Actions
Maximize State Growth	To encourage state development, expanding firms, or firms moving in, are offered public infrastructure, tax breaks, low interest loans, and other incentives.
Income Redistribution	State goals are similar to federal goals in this respect, and the relevant policies are outlined above. However, states are limited in their ability to redistribute income because households and businesses unwilling to pay for redistributive programs can move to less progressive states.
Economic Stabilization	Again, state goals correspond to national goals, but may differ markedly in their timing and intensity. Even during the recent, deep national recession, some states experienced only a shallow recession, and differed in the timing of their downturns and troughs. For example, while the construction industry experienced a deep recession nationally, the construction slump was, proportionately, less significant in growing areas such as Texas and Southern California. Thus countercyclical needs, both in timing and volume, differed among states. The federal response—the Local Public Works Program—took little account of these differences, and often created local construction bottlenecks (Vernez and Vaughan, 1978).
Intrastate Distribution of Economic Activity	States are also concerned with the distribution of economic activity *within* their borders. They attempt to encourage the

industry in distressed areas. Throughout the 1960s these efforts tended to be oriented toward rural areas, although the recent emphasis has been on central cities. To target expansion, states may offer fiscal assistance to distressed jurisdictions, locate state facilities where unemployment is high, build industrial parks, offer tax incentives, provide training programs, give low interest loans, or even prohibit local tax incentives in rapidly growing areas.

There are some obvious conflicts between state and national goals. First, and perhaps most important, the state goal of encouraging local growth may conflict with the national goal of balanced regional growth. Successful attempts by states to entice businesses away from other states may exacerbate interstate growth differentials. One state's gain is frequently another's loss. However, to the extent that a relocation allows a company to construct a more efficient plant and take advantage of better public infrastructure, national productivity may be enhanced. Overall, interstate competition is not productive. States in the Northeast have suffered under federal policies designed to raise the level of economic development in the low-income South. In fact, any federal regional strategy is bound to affect adversely economic development in non-target states unless the federal strategy addresses real market failure problems and succeeds in increasing total investment and employment so that all areas can gain.

A second conflict revolves around stabilization policy. The federal emphasis during the recent recession on construction activity—typified by the $6 billion Local Public Works Program—ran up against relatively tight construction markets in some states. Even in upstate New York, scarcely a booming construction area, there are reports that the construction schedule for the 1980 Winter Olympics facilities at Lake Placid was jeopardized by a lack of heavy construction firms able to bid as a result of their participation in a number of Local Public Works projects.

A third conflict is less obvious but just as important. Federal programs aimed at social goals may inadvertently slow development in some states. There is some evidence to suggest that abating pollution or enforcing safety and health conditions slow growth more in older central cities, where it is difficult to modify plant and equipment, than in faster growing areas. State officials must always be aware that a federal policy may have very different regional impacts, even though *16* it is enforced nationwide.

Local Goals   Local jurisdictions have a set of goals
                         similar to states, although applicable to
their own smaller boundaries.

The most important area of potential conflict between states and
local jurisdictions is between the state goal of balanced growth and the
desire of many jurisdictions to maximize their own growth rate. Local
jurisdictions can offer business tax incentives that attract businesses
from distressed urban centers within the state.[4] City/suburban tax
differentials have played an important role in encouraging the
suburbanization of jobs and households. This process is not necessarily desirable, for it can force a state government into the contra-
dictory position of helping its suburban areas to accommodate business expansion and its central cities to redevelop abandoned facilities.

A second area of potential conflict is between the state's goal of
assisting the poor and the desire of more affluent local jurisdictions
to avoid redistributive taxes. The suburbanization of the nation's
urban population has been accomplished through the proliferation of
relatively homogeneous suburban communities that offer residents
respite from central city tax burdens. These communities may not
welcome increased state taxes that are channeled back into central
cities. Until the last few years, this conflict has resulted in a marked
unwillingness by state governments to involve themselves in the plight
of central cities.

Another point of potential conflict occurs over the use of federal
categorical and formula grants. Now that local areas are recipients of
substantial amounts of federal funds for capital projects, the state can
no longer ensure that local plans are coordinated—either with each
other or with the state's own overall plan for state-funded projects.
For example, a UDAG-financed shopping mall may not be effectively
sited within the context of state transportation plans.

IMPLICATIONS

Two major conclusions can be drawn
from this discussion. First, state eco-
nomic development programs are undertaken in response to perceived
problems—problems of place, people, or jurisdiction. The diagnosis
of the causes of economic development problems—reflected in slow
growth, high unemployment, and other familiar symptoms—affects
the type of strategy implemented, and tax policy has a role within
strategies aimed at each class of problems. But tax policy is only one
weapon in an extensive armory of development policies. Other state
actions include shifting program priorities, redesigning the geographic distribution of expenditures, and regulation of economic
activity and local fiscal practices. The following chapter outlines the
basic considerations that should guide state development policy
makers in the design of their tax policies.   *17*

The second, more obvious conclusion is that there are clear conflicts between federal, state and local economic development goals. The principal conflicts between federal and state goals occur in the areas of balanced growth, income redistribution, and the inadvertent effects of broad federal social programs on local economies. State/local conflicts occur over interjurisdictional competition for growth, and in coordinating state and local development plans. As we shall see, these conflicts extend into the design and implementation of state tax policies.

FOOTNOTES TO CHAPTER 1

1. A major distinction between the problems of jurisdiction and the problems of place is that the severity of the former would be affected by changes in jurisdictional boundaries, while the latter would not.

2. Poor states well-endowed with such natural resources as lumber, iron ore, oil, natural gas, or coal have the best opportunity for this through severance taxes. But so do states with a substantial tourist trade or many out-of-state commuters.

3. A great deal has been written about state surpluses. Gramlich (1978) has argued that the rapid build up of surpluses since 1976 has acted to frustrate federal expansionary economic policy. However, as Stanfield (1978) has pointed out, it is difficult to determine the size of these surpluses from national income accounts published in the *Survey of Current Business*. Some surpluses represent offsets against pension obligations.

4. The discussion of business taxes in Chapter 5 suggests that intrastate variations are greater than interstate variations, and that tax differences have affected interstate business relocations more than interstate moves.

WHAT FACTORS INFLUENCE ECONOMIC DEVELOPMENT?

In trying to unravel the complex process of economic development to identify how state and local taxes may be influential, two facts stand out. First, *state and local taxes are only one factor among many that directly influence development, and, in fact, are not a major factor.* The role of taxes is not discussed in this chapter, but is discussed in detail in the following chapters. The discussion in this chapter provides a context in which to view the role of taxes. Second, *many of the ways in which taxes shape the development process are indirect.* For example, taxes affect residential location decisions which, in turn, affect the local demand for goods and services. A tax policy that attracted middle- and upper-income households would contribute to local development.

COMPONENTS OF EMPLOYMENT CHANGE[1]

Areas suffering from high unemployment often blame their difficulties on the out-migration of firms, and regard as a panacea an aggressive promotional campaign to attract new footloose firms. The myth of a rich vein of large, non-polluting firms that can be mined by state development officials offering free land and access roads, subsidized buildings, and tax abatements, has distorted state development efforts for years. A rational economic development policy cannot be developed until this myth is dispelled and the true components of employment change are identified. Recent studies on the location of industrial firms has revealed the following:

■ Interregional migration of firms is the least important component of employment change.[2] Differences in birth rates and the rate of expansion of existing firms are much more important. There is very little regional variation in the rate at which jobs are lost through firm contractions or closures.
■ Firm moves are slightly more important in determining central city/suburban growth differences, but are still less important than other components.
■ The birth rate of new firms is much higher in suburban locations than in central cities. Central cities do *not* tend to act as incubators. **19**

■ New, closing, and locally moving firms are smaller than stationary firms.
■ Most new jobs in an area are created by the expansion of employment in relatively small, young, and independent firms.

What are the implications of these findings for development policy? Unfortunately, we don't yet know what factors affect each of the components of employment change, so it is difficult to target policies. Obviously, research in this crucial area should continue. We can say that any continued effort to chase smokestacks is probably misplaced, and that greater effort should be devoted to ensuring that the overall economic environment is as attractive as possible, rather than simply providing benefits to a few large firms. The remainder of this chapter examines the factors that influence development.

Factors that influence growth and development may be separated into three types: those that affect the demand for output; those that affect the cost of production at a particular location; and a less tangible group of amenities that may affect the attractiveness of a particular location as a place to live and do business, such as air quality, recreation facilities, and the crime rate. The last group may affect the local market and local costs, but they do so less directly than the other factors.

Demand
Consumer market: population and income
Intermediate market: interindustry linkages

Input Costs and Availability
Transportation
Labor: size of force, skill level, wages, productivity, unionization
Land
Raw materials
Energy
Finance
Taxes and municipal services
External economies: scale and agglomeration

Local Characteristics
Amenities
Leadership

It is extremely difficult to separate the effects of these different factors and weigh them according to their relative impact on changing patterns of economic activity. For example, it seems probable that one factor in the rapid expansion of manufacturing activity in the South was the extension of the federal highway system into areas of declining agricultural employment where there was a ready pool of surplus labor. Should the rapid growth in that region be attributed to reduced transportation costs or to low-cost labor? The introduction of air conditioning for manufacturing plants may also have stimulated economic development in the South. How should the Southern growth rate be attributed among these three factors?

Another problem is that it is difficult to measure the factors themselves. For example, wages do not measure the skill of the labor force or the hiring and training costs a firm must incur.

Since state economic development policy is concerned with both aggregate economic growth and its distribution within the state, the following discussion analyzes how these determinants have influenced *interregional and intraregional* growth patterns.

CONSUMER MARKET

There is considerable evidence that market considerations are the most important single factor in explaining interstate differences in economic development, and that growth in employment follows rather than leads growth in population.[3]

Separating the influence of the level of demand on employment in an area is difficult. The size of the local population, often used as an index of demand, also measures the availability of labor. Demand, output and employment interact in a complex way, as shown in Figure 1. Growth in local population leads to an increase in both labor supply and the demand for output, leading to an increase in demand for labor. The growth in labor demand stimulates the increase in population as migrants arrive seeking jobs. As employment increases, so does local income, which stimulates a further increase in demand (the multiplier effect). Within this dynamic system it is difficult to determine whether growth in market demand stimulates the growth in employment or whether the growth in employment opportunities attracts people. Undoubtedly, the relative strength of the two effects differs from place to place. Retired persons seeking the sun in Phoenix or Miami are little interested in jobs, although their purchasing power has attracted businesses to these cities. Auto workers were attracted to Detroit by job opportunities.

There is some consensus that the expansion of local markets through population and income growth is the single most important factor in encouraging employment growth.

There is also some evidence that jobs have followed people to the suburbs. Using pooled cross-sectional and time series data for 15 SMSAs, Steinnes (1977, p. 76) found that, for both manufacturing and service jobs, businesses followed household location rather than the reverse. In fact, he found that people tended to move away from **21**

Figure 1
The Relationship Between Population, Labor Force,
and Employment in a Local Area.

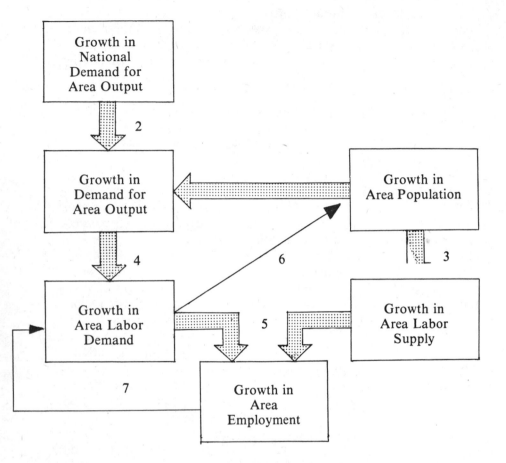

LINKAGES:

1. Population growth leads to expanded local market for goods and services and increased size leads to increased import substitution.

2. National growth leads to expanded local market for goods and services.

3. Population growth leads to increased local labor supply.

4. Increased demand for local goods and services leads to increased demand for labor.

5. Increased labor demand and supply lead to increased output.

6. Growth in demand for labor encourages population inmigration.

7. Increased output leads to increased local income causing an increase in local demand.

manufacturing jobs, presumably because of pollution or other dis-amenities. He concluded that "the efforts of central cities to attract and retain manufacturing may be accelerating, not retarding, the flight of residents from the city."

INTERMEDIATE MARKETS

The level of employment in their prin-cipal buyers is an important locational determinant for industries whose chief market is other industries. In addition, the presence of industries that provide vital inputs will make an area attractive to some industries. In a detailed analysis of output growth in 84 industries, Harris and Hopkins (1972) found that 32 industries were significantly influenced by the output growth of major customers. For example, the petroleum refining industry tended to locate close to the petroleum extraction industry (a major supplier), and the metal containers industry tended to locate near the beverages industry (a major buyer). Overall, evidence suggests that reduced transportation costs have reduced the necessity of locating near supplying industries and have made firms more footloose. The present gasoline shortage may reverse this ten-dency.

TRANSPORTATION

Transportation costs affect both the reve-nue a firm receives from its sales and the prices it must pay for its inputs. It is difficult to separate these two components in most of the studies that have been conducted. Lichten-berg (1960) estimated that 51 percent of manufacturing industries were sensitive to changes in transportation costs. Of these, 84 percent were sensitive to the costs of transporting commodities to consumers, and only 16 percent were sensitive to the costs of transporting inputs. Harris and Hopkins (1972) also found that more firms were sensitive to output transportation costs than to input costs.

Costs of transporting commodities to consumers have been affected by the rapid growth of trucking. The share of trucking in total freight transportation rose from 9.5 percent in 1940 to 21.3 percent in 1970, the increase coming almost entirely at the expense of the railroads. Truck transportation reduces the cost of small-load, short-haul freight movements relative to large-load, long-haul movements (Chinitz and Vernon, 1960) and has led to decentralization of industry as firms moved toward highway linkages and away from railroads. The growth of trucking has also increased the tendency for firms to locate near the market for their products. Cities with businesses using short-haul, small-load transportation[4] and able to relocate wherever there are trucking facilities will experience a more rapid loss of employment than cities whose industries rely on heavy-load, long-haul trans-portation.[5]

Many older cities that developed around rail terminals are ill-equipped to make the transition to truck transportation. Building densities are high and access inadequate. Congestion is heavy and parking spaces and truck terminals too few and too small. Firms may have moved away from older cities to escape these problems. Boston, New York, Baltimore, and Philadelphia—which have traditionally housed a large number of small firms whose products are fairly transportation-intensive—have been unable to compete with newer, truck-oriented cities.

In addition, the rapid growth in the use of private automobiles for commuting has increased the cost of transporting labor to work relative to the cost of transporting materials (Moses and Williamson, 1967). When the transportation costs of materials were of prime importance, companies located on railroad spurs in the central city. With the increase in labor force commuting costs, companies have tended to relocate closer to their labor supply.[6] For companies requiring skilled labor, this means a move to the suburbs. Companies requiring unskilled labor, which is less mobile than skilled labor, tend to remain or relocate within the city because of the availability of public transportation for their work force.

LABOR

Labor is the most important single factor of production. Nearly half of the value added in manufacturing in 1972 was spent on payrolls. Two-thirds of these payrolls were for production workers. Among the many dimensions of the labor input into the production process that are relevant to industrial growth process and location decisions are:

■ *The size of the unskilled labor market pool.* A company that experiences considerable seasonal or cyclical fluctuations in demand needs to be located in an area with a large labor pool that will allow it to hire easily in times of need (the apparel industry in New York is one example). Companies tend to lay off unskilled workers during a recession more readily than skilled workers.

■ *The skill level of the labor force.* Training labor can be expensive, so an area that already has a supply of skilled labor will be an attractive location. Labor priced low relative to its skill has been a major factor in the development of manfacturing in the South. To some extent, low wages in the South reflect low local taxes. However, rapid development in the South and slow growth in the North has narrowed wage differences and absorbed much of the surplus labor in the South. Future regional growth differentials are unlikely to be as pronounced as those in the past.

■ *Unionization.* It has been argued that companies move to avoid high

wages and expensive working conditions imposed by powerful unions.

Evidence suggests that the main influence of unionization is on wages and not on any induced labor negotiation problems or work stoppages. Regional growth differences have been associated with a reduction in private sector unionization in the North and an increase in the South.

■ *Racial composition of labor force.* It has been argued that companies relocate to avoid having to hire minority employees—a business parallel to residential "white flight." There is no evidence to support this allegation.

LAND

Although a shortage of low-price land in central cities and in the Northeastern states in general has often been advanced as a reason for the decline in manufacturing activity in those areas, there is little evidence to substantiate this view (Harrison, 1974). Measuring the availability of land in an urban area is a difficult task. Land embodies many locational factors that may or may not be important to a company, depending upon its factor requirements. Square footage is not the only consideration in the purchase or lease of land. The purchaser is interested in the availability of transportation linkages, the ease with which trucks can make deliveries and collections, and the proximity of a railroad spur or a shipping pier. He is also concerned with the safety of the neighborhood, what precautions must be taken to minimize losses due to theft and vandalism, and the security necessary to protect his work force. The local red tape involved in site assembly may be a much greater investment barrier than either the quantity or price of land.

RAW MATERIALS

Proximity to raw materials, once a major determinant of the location of several manufacturing sectors, has declined in importance. As Niedercorn and Kain (1963, p. 130) explain:

> This is an inevitable concomitant to the later stages of economic development because value added by labor and capital becomes a larger and larger proportion of the total value of output. Today's complex products require much more processing per unit of raw material than those of a generation ago. So, location near the source of raw materials no longer gives an area a decisive advantage in many branches of manufacturing, because raw material costs have become a smaller fraction of total costs.

Raw materials may affect location within urban areas in a different way. Handling raw materials encourages firms that use them extensively to seek a suburban rather than a central city location so as to minimize the costs of constructing land-intensive truck-loading facilities and warehousing. Although the effect is weak, the tendency is perceptible (Kemper, 1974).

ENERGY

Recent international developments have made the energy sector and the effects of federal energy policy areas of considerable importance. In 1974, manufacturing used one-third of all energy consumed in the United States.

Energy costs vary regionally; the most expensive energy is in the Northeast, the cheapest in the West. Research has indicated that energy prices do influence growth (Huntington and Kahn, 1976).

Probably of greater importance than interstate variations in energy prices has been the impact of federal regulations that have placed producing states at a distinct advantage over non-producing states. Jones (1975, p. 1) summarizes:

> Constraints on gas supply, brought about by price regulation, have discouraged any expansion in regional gas consumption, however, and the Northeast has experienced extensive curtailment of industrial and commercial customers.

FINANCE

The availability and cost of finance are important factors in economic development. There has been very little research into the effects that differences in regional capital markets may have on different growth rates. It is usually assumed that the capital market is a national market and that all borrowers face similar interest rates and loan availability. The banking industry, however, is heavily regulated at both the state and federal levels (Gardner, 1973). This regulation may influence interest rate differentials, which in turn influence local growth rates. For example, mortgage usury ceilings have exacerbated cycles in residential construction during inflationary periods. Also, federal regulation of pension funds and of venture capital corporations has reduced the supply of equity capital. Recent changes have ameliorated—but not cured—this problem.

Other aspects of bank credit deserve attention. The interest rate alone does not reflect the availability of credit. Entry into the banking field is quite severely restricted. Peltzman (1965) estimated that there were 50 percent fewer new banks than there would have been in the absence of such regulation. Pakonen (1971) found that the entry rates were reduced even further in unit-banking states. Restricted entry allows banks to discriminate among loan applications so as to minimize risk. Gardner (1973) found that banks in St. Louis behave much more conservatively than they would in the presence of more competition. Clearly, this risk-averse behavior can dampen growth by causing new companies to shift to more congenial areas.

MUNICIPAL SERVICES

The role of public services in industrial location is more difficult to assess than the role of taxes. The effectiveness of municipal services can influence the crime rate, the level of amenities, the overall atmosphere in which business is conducted, the quality of neighborhood schools, and the quality of the air. The only insight into the role of the quality of municipal services has come from questionnaires and surveys. The Economic Development Administration (1971) found that fire and police protection were the two community attributes most frequently cited by business as being of prime importance in location decisions. In the survey conducted by Hartnett (1972), services were ranked thirteenth (out of 23) among *vitally important* factors and tenth among *important* factors. Several public service-related factors were also listed, including "the condition of the neighborhood" and "zoning."

An interesting insight into another aspect of municipal services and the role of local government emerges from Hartnett's survey. He asked firms what they felt the city could do to improve the business climate. There were 117 responses. The city should: train labor (10), offer financial incentives (9), purchase its supplies from industries located in the city (3), reduce taxes (31), reduce the number of rules and regulations (8), cut red tape (10), end harassment by city inspectors (21), reduce time lost from inspection visits (6), and improve its attitude (11). The fact that regulations, red tape, harassment, inspection time, and attitude accounted for 56 of the responses, compared with 40 concerning taxes and financial incentives, shows the potential importance of aspects of municipal behavior that have received little attention.

EXTERNAL ECONOMIES

Urban researchers have long hypothesized that companies may receive certain advantages by locating in a large urban area, advantages that result from processes external to the individual company but that can reduce the cost or improve the productivity of labor when the company does business there. Highly industrialized states, with diverse bases and large labor forces, may offer advantages to some industries that cannot be found in less urban states. By identifying those industries or even types of firms that seem to be especially attracted by agglomeration economies, state urban development policies can be tailored to them and be made more effective. Further, substantial agglomeration economies imply that the process of decline in employment in some urban areas will be self-sustaining. If firms move out of the city or substantially reduce their level of **27** employment, then the economies of agglomeration, and, therefore, the competitive position of remaining companies, will be impaired.

AMENITIES

The quality of life—the availability of recreational and cultural facilities, the cleanliness of the environment, the freedom from congestion and crime, and the quality of local schools—is an important consideration in the location decisions of some companies. If a firm is not tied to a large labor pool, raw materials, or rail or water linkages, then the attractiveness of a location as a place to live may play an important role.

The most important effect of differential levels of amenities is on the migration patterns of households. Executives may encourage the relocation of their company to an area they find attractive as a place to live. Amenities may also provide a small monetary incentive for relocation. Workers who live in pleasant, unpolluted, and uncongested surroundings will accept lower wages (Izraeli, 1973). Thus state environmental, cultural and recreational programs can be an influential economic development tool.

In one study, Burns and Pang (1977) separately analyzed factors that had influenced the movement of corporate headquarters between cities and from central cities to suburbs. Their conclusion is that suburban moves are influenced by major expense factors, while intercity moves reflect a desire to improve the level of community amenities. There is little, if these results are to be believed, that states or localities can do to influence overall state development through fiscal inducements, *although they may be able to influence intrastate development patterns through targeted inducements.*

LEADERSHIP

Leadership, both civic and entrepreneurial, is one of the most nebulous, yet also one of the most important, factors in explaining shifting patterns of economic development. The topic has been an issue among economic historians for many years. Thompson (1965), in an anecdotal description of the fates of three cities, provides an excellent introduction to the subject. He describes the adjustment of Boston to the loss of employment in the footwear industry, once a major industry. Leadership, civic and private, he surmises, may have been important in developing the research industry as a substitute. He also discusses the importance of leadership in the emergence of Chicago, rather than St. Louis, as the dominant Midwestern city.

The importance of individuals, as city leaders or as leaders of private institutions, in the adaptation of a city to changing economic conditions is difficult to assess. Was it far-sighted administrators in

municipal government and local universities who led Boston to recovery from the extensive unemployment it faced at the end of World War II? Has the failure of some cities to diversify and capture growth industries resulted from their inadequate pool of natural endowments, from a failure of civic leaders to pursue an effective economic development policy, or from the failure of the policies themselves? In informal surveys, the attitude of local officials appears quite frequently as an important determinant of locational choice.

IMPLICATIONS[7]

This brief discussion of the factors that shape economic development has provided a number of important lessons that should be borne in mind when shaping state tax policies for economic development. The basic links between some of these factors, state development policies, and taxes are shown in Table 1. The major guidelines for a state economic development policy are:

■ *Combine improvements to the residential environment with improvements to the business climate.* The artificial distinction between community development and economic development ignores the symbiotic relationship between population growth and employment growth. Unless skilled workers, scientists and entrepreneurs can provide both a market and a supply of labor, an economic development program is bound to be ineffectual. Thus personal taxes are as much a development tool as business taxes.

■ *The future cannot be extrapolated from the past.* The very factors that give a particular state a comparative advantage during one period are eroded by differential rates of development. Wages and prices have climbed faster in the rapidly growing Sunbelt than in the slowly growing North. Home prices in booming Southern California make a move from Baltimore to Los Angeles, even at a substantial salary increase, a difficult proposition. Over time, the market system will come to the aid of declining areas, if state and federal policies allow it.

■ *Concentrate upon developing an attractive business environment, not upon offering special favors to a few companies.* Most employment growth must come from the expansion of existing companies, particularly relatively small ones, and from new births. These companies are often immune to the benefits of a personalized development program.

■ *Concentrate upon developing an equitable tax system that is tailored neither to the special interests of the existing structure nor to attracting a special class of footloose industries.* There are few footloose industries upon which to draw, and location decisions are based upon many factors, among which taxes play only a small role.

■ *Tax incentives do not define the business climate.* An economic   **29**

Table 1
Factors Influencing State Development,
Related State Development Policies, and the Role of Taxes

Factor	State Development Policies	State Tax Policy
Consumer Markets	• Residential amenities • Public service delivery • Housing programs	• Personal income and property taxes • Distressed areas can be aided by increased fiscal equalization efforts by the states • Tax treatment of out-of-state sales and production
Labor	• Public employment and training programs • Right-to-Work laws • Wage regulation	• Payroll and personal taxes affect wages • Tax incentives for training • Personal income taxes influencing labor force participation
Transportation	• Highway, road, and rail programs • Freight regulation • Mass transit subsidies	• Property taxes on transportation facilities
Land	• Land assembly grants • Land use regulations	• Depreciation provisions • Capital gains taxes • Property tax rates
Energy	• Public Utility Commissions • Public ownership • Land use regulation • Environmental regulation	• Utility sales taxes • Property taxes • Severance taxes • Depletion allowances
Capital	• Banking regulation • Public finance corporations	• Tax exempt bonds • Depreciation allowances • Corporate income taxes
Amenities	• Environmental regulation • Recreational programs • Subsidies to the arts	• Tax exempt pollution abatement bonds • Tax deductible business expenses • Tax treatment of not-for profit institutions

development policy must proceed on a number of coordinated fronts. Upgrading the quality of the labor force, ensuring adequate transportation links, adequate public infrastructure, facilitating land assembly, and reducing local red tape are much more important components, and much more influential when offered in combination, than tax holidays.

FOOTNOTES TO CHAPTER 2

1. For a review of the studies of employment change, see Allaman and Birch, 1975; Birch, 1978; Ledebur, 1978; and an excellent synthesis by Wolman, 1978.

2. This is very different from population growth. Although interarea differences in births and deaths explain a small part of interarea differences in population growth, *migration explains most of these differences.*

3. See Vaughan, 1977; and Vaughan and Vogel, 1979.

4. These industries may include apparel, food processing, printing and publishing, and specialized durable goods.

5. These industries may include primary metals and heavy equipment.

6. The incentive to do so comes from the fact that a company moving to the suburbs may offer its workers lower wages since the work force will spend less time traveling. If the work force is unionized so that wages are equalized throughout the metropolitan area, no such savings will be enjoyed though the company may find it easier to hire in the suburbs).

7. These implications anticipate some of the conclusions from the following chapters.

GUIDELINES
FOR DEVELOPING
A STATE TAX POLICY

What should guide the development of state tax policies? Three basic considerations must shape the way we evaluate existing tax policies: efficiency, equity, and administrative cost. This chapter explores these three concepts and discusses how they can provide a basis for selecting an appropriate tax structure. It also explores the constraints upon state tax policy imposed by: 1) the role of the state in the federal fiscal structure; 2) the problem of fiscal strain; and 3) our lack of knowledge concerning the impacts and incidence of taxes.

EFFICIENCY   In trying to construct an *efficient* tax system we are concerned with minimizing the disruptive effects of raising revenues to support state services. How can a tax system be disruptive? First, and at present the most fashionable of fiscal concerns, the *level* of taxation may be too high, and stifle economic expansion. Broadly speaking, this means that the value of additional state supported services tends to be valued well below their cost in terms of the necessary local tax payments. Second, the *structure* of the tax system may cause inefficient behavior on the part of taxpayers. For example, a personal income tax, because it taxes wages, leads to reduced labor force participation, an efficiency loss. A property tax may discourage the upgrading of real property. The tax structure may also lead to spatial inefficiencies—failure to treat land as a depreciable asset leads firms to select sites in urban fringe areas where values can be expected to appreciate, encouraging urban sprawl. What characteristics must a state tax system have in order to achieve the greatest efficiency?

First, the level of taxes should be consonant with the local preference for state-provided public services. This does not mean that taxes must be as low as possible. The residents of some states, such as New York and Massachusetts, have long shown a preference for more public services than residents of other states. However, public officials have too long taken an annual increase in state public employment and activities as a matter of course, and the budgeting review procedure has been far too soft. The result has been a steady deterioration in fiscal conditions that the mid-1970s recession cast in stark relief. States should question proposed increases much more severely than they are used to, and should avoid a tax system whose levels are way out of line with those in neighboring states.

Second, the structure of state taxes should not actively discriminate against actions which benefit economic development. Unfortunately, most taxes cause some loss of economic efficiency. A tax on earned income discourages labor force participation, and a tax on the income from capital discourages investment. A tax increase in one jurisdiction may cause businesses to move elsewhere, although the move yields no real efficiency gain. The only tax that avoids any efficiency loss is a lump sum head tax, and that violates all considerations of equity. We cannot hope, therefore, to build a perfectly efficient state tax system. But we can hope to improve on the level of efficiency of the present system.

EQUITY

The desire to make a state's tax structure as fair as possible yields three principles. *First, all other factors being equal, the greater a household or firm's resources, the greater the amount of taxes it should pay.* This is referred to as vertical equity. Resources may refer either to a stock— *wealth*—or to the flow of *income* generated by that stock. Whether the amount of taxes should increase proportionately to resources is a major and recurring fiscal issue. But we should note that those who advocate a progressive tax on income or wealth are not necessarily advocating that the tax burden increase more than proportionately to resources. They often argue that non-taxed resources are greater for those with high incomes than for those less well-off, and, therefore, a progressive income tax leads to an increase in tax burden proportional to the increase in resources.

Second, those with similar resources should pay similar amounts of tax. This is referred to as horizontal equity. All other things being equal, the tax burdens for similarly endowed households should not differ according to location, race, age or other characteristics. This does not imply that any geographical variation in tax rates is inequitable. One jurisdiction may offer a lower level of public services—fewer parks and libraries, or less police protection. The fact that taxes in these areas are lower than in a jurisdiction with extensive public services is not inequitable.

The final equity criterion is that, all other things being equal, *the greater the volume of public services received by a taxpayer, the greater the amount of taxes he should pay.* A firm taking intensive advantage of locally provided roads, water supply, and sewers, should pay more in taxes and fees than a similarly endowed firm that uses less truck transportation, uses little water, and discharges no waste.

ADMINISTRATIVE COST

Collecting taxes is not without cost. Taxpayers are all too familiar with the burden of completing the alphabet soup of tax forms, or paying an accountant to do it for them. States must process these tax statements and identify and prosecute those illegally avoiding taxes. But there are other costs as well. A tax that fails to yield an expected revenue necessitates hasty service cut-backs at considerable human and administrative cost. A tax whose revenue does not grow as service demand expands must constantly be readjusted, inducing uncertainty and expensive political deliberations. And finally, a tax should exert some countercyclical influence. Revenues should fall as economic activity declines, and grow as it grows. There are, therefore, four administrative principles, summarized in Table 2, together with efficiency and equity criteria.

It is apparent that these criteria are not necessarily mutually consistent. Efficiency may be improved at the expense of equity. A predictable tax revenue may not be cyclically stabilizing. However, these contradictions may be resolvable because the criteria in Table 2 are those desired of the tax system as a whole—all taxes taken together. An inequitable but efficient tax may be balanced by another less efficient but more equitable tax.

CONSTRAINTS ON STATE TAX POLICY: FISCAL FEDERALISM

Unfortunately, we cannot simply apply these criteria to current state fiscal practices. States operate within a federal fiscal structure that determines both how state taxes act upon firms and households, and the public service responsibilities that the state must meet.

The Federal Role

Federal influence over state and local fiscal matters has advanced on six fronts. First, public revenue collection is increasingly a federal function. Thus states acting alone are less able to shape the overall tax system. In 1902, Washington collected only 19 percent of revenues for civil functions, and made only 18.5 percent of all civil expenditures. By 1977, over 50 percent of civil revenues were collected in Washington, although less than one quarter of civil expenditures were made by federal agencies. The federal fiscal structure originally allocated to each layer of government a different tax base and different responsibilities. The federal government claimed personal income taxes and business taxes, and was responsible for national defense and major internal development issues. The state government collected sales taxes and governed state issues such as transportation and criminal justice. Local governments relied upon the property tax and administered education, health and local roads. The rapid growth of the public sector, reces-

Table 2
Criteria for Designing State Tax Policy

Efficiency
- The overall burden of taxes should reflect local preferences for public services.
- The tax structure should not lead to undesirable actions by taxpayers such as firm and household relocation.

Equity
- The greater a taxpayer's resources, the greater the tax burden (vertical equity).
- Taxpayers with similar resources should pay similar tax burdens, all other things being equal (horizontal equity).
- The tax burden for taxpayers with similar resources should be related to the value of public services received.

Administrative Ease
- The tax should be simple to collect and enforce.
- The tax revenue should be predictable.
- The tax revenue should grow secularly with the local demand for public services and the level of economic activity.
- The tax revenue should be cyclically stabilizing.

---

sions, and wars have melted the layer cake of fiscal federalism, blurring distinctions of revenue sources and responsibilities. Table 3 shows the source of funding for selected state and local functions. State governments are dominant in education, highways and health. Local government efforts are concentrated on criminal justice, education and health. And federal responsibility is for welfare and highways.

Second, the federal government shapes the way state taxes are collected. For example, the federal tax code allows local taxes to be deducted from federal taxable income. This has discouraged state and local governments from relying on fees and charges which are not deductible. In addition, Internal Revenue Service practices—the definitions of gross and taxable income, for example—provide a model that is difficult for state tax collectors to avoid.

Third, by distributing more and more resources through intergovernmental grants—grants that carry powerful, behavior modifying strings—the federal government, increasingly, is controlling how state and local expenditures are made. The way formula grants are

Table 3
Source of Funding for Selected Major Functions of
State and Local Governments
(FY 1977)

Function	State and Local Expenditures ($ Billions)	Federal Aid	Percentage from State Government	Local Government
Education	102.8	9.9	52.5	37.6
Public Welfare	34.5	56.5	38.3	5.2
Highways	23.1	26.4	49.4	24.2
Health & Hospitals	22.5	10.7	44.0	45.3
Police Protection	11.7	7.2	29.1	63.7

SOURCE: U.S. Bureau of the Census, *Governmental Finances 1976-77,* Washington, D.C.
  · 1978.

distributed affects local actions. General Revenue Sharing allocations are based, in part, on local tax efforts, and Community Development Block Grant allocations are tied to efforts to provide local public housing. The result is that no discussion of state taxation policies is complete without reference to federal policies.

Fourth, the proportion of federal aid that bypasses states and flows directly to local government units has increased dramatically. The Housing Act of 1937 was the first that enabled the federal government to give funds directly to local governments. Recently, CETA funds, now totalling $5 billion per annum, and the massive $6 billion counter-recessionary Local Public Works Program, as well as General and Antirecessionary Revenue Sharing, have also, in large part, bypassed the states. These flows of federal funds affect state and local tax rates, the degree to which local service needs can be met, and the power of the state to influence local conditions.

Fifth, federal legislation has mandated programs that range from clean drinking water to assistance for the disabled. Meeting federal standards often necessitates considerable local expenditures and, therefore, increases in local tax rates. Complying with federal requirements leaves state and local governments with less and less discretionary power over their own expenditures.

A final avenue of federal influence has been through court decisions affirming civil rights and equality of opportunity. Most significant among these was the *Serrano vs. Priest* decision in California, and its repercussions in other states.[1] Courts have found that reliance on the local property tax for the bulk of support of public education is discriminatory, and that current state education aid denies equal protection of the law to local school children. A massive shift in the tax burden from jurisdictions to the state will be required to comply with these decisions. This will probably necessitate a reduced reliance on the property tax.

State/Local Relations   In judging the effectiveness of state tax policy we must be aware that states differ markedly in their relations with local jurisdictions. For example, in New York, the state government collects only 48 percent of the total state/local tax revenues and makes only a quarter of the direct expenditures. By contrast, the state of Hawaii collects 78.6 percent of the tax revenues and makes 76.6 percent of the expenditures. Table 4 shows tax revenues and direct expenditures by state and local governments in FY 1977. All other things being equal, the lower the share of total state/local spending by the state government, the less influence on economic development that government can exert through tax and expenditure programs without the cooperation of local units.

As well as paying directly for some part of local services, state governments help local areas meet their fiscal objectives in four ways: (1) they issue grants to equalize fiscal capacity; (2) they authorize locally administered taxes; (3) they authorize local supplements to state taxes; and (4) they implement tax sharing. The effectiveness of these actions in improving the state/local fiscal structure is examined in the following chapter.

CONSTRAINTS ON STATE TAX POLICY: FISCAL CONDITIONS[2]   The fiscal actions of state governments are not limited only by the structure of fiscal federalism, but also by the resources and preferences of their residents. The unwillingness of many taxpayers to finance ever-growing state and local budgets has compelled local politicians to make unpopular decisions to cut back local services. An inability to balance budgets and the unacceptability of massive layoffs and service cuts has confronted many troubled cities with "fiscal crises," crises that are often quickly transmitted to the state government. A definition of "fiscal crisis" has remained elusive.

The fiscal strength of a state or local area, in both absolute and relative terms, is an important concept. Fiscal strength affects the ease with which the state may enter the bond market, and the way in which federal funds are distributed. The fiscal strength of the state of California, measured by its large surplus in FY 1978, encouraged the pas-

Table 4
Selected Items of State and Local Government Finances
by Level of Government: 1976-77
(Dollar amounts in millions)

State	Tax revenue			Direct general expenditure			State government percentage of —	
	Total	State government	Local governments	Total	State government	Local governments	Tax revenue	Direct general expenditure
United States	175 878.7	101 084.6	74 794.0	273 001.8	103 535.0	169 466.7	57.5	37.9
Alabama.......	1 870.7	1 403.7	467.0	3 696.3	1 862.1	1 834.2	75.0	50.4
Alaska........	934.4	773.5	160.9	1 333.1	793.8	539.2	82.8	59.6
Arizona........	1 897.8	1 160.1	737.8	2 853.4	964.4	1 889.0	61.1	33.8
Arkansas	1 059.3	802.9	256.4	1 878.6	947.5	931.0	75.8	50.4
California......	23 842.9	12 589.1	11 253.8	32 532.1	9 942.0	22 590.1	52.8	30.6
Colorado	2 157.6	1 077.3	1 060.3	3 524.6	1 268.6	2 256.0	49.9	36.5
Connecticut	2 750.0	1 457.1	1 293.8	3 579.3	1 607.0	1 972.3	53.9	44.9
Delaware	482.7	390.9	91.8	848.7	474.4	374.3	81.0	55.1
D.C.	738.7	(X)	738.7	1 424.0	(X)	1 424.0	(X)	(X)
Florida	5 309.2	3 274.8	2 034.4	9 287.5	2 886.0	6 401.5	61.7	31.1
Georgia........	3 074.7	1 906.5	1 168.2	5 060.9	2 121.3	2 939.6	62.0	41.9
Hawaii	872.1	685.7	186.4	1 714.1	1 313.5	400.6	78.6	76.6
Idaho	547.9	367.8	180.1	977.7	464.1	513.6	67.1	47.5
Illinois.........	9 674.0	5 319.5	4 354.4	14 237.0	5 703.8	8 533.1	55.0	40.1
Indiana	3 477.6	2 162.9	1 314.7	5 080.1	1 851.5	3 228.6	62.2	36.4
Iowa	2 155.2	1 292.5	862.7	3 556.3	1 391.8	2 164.4	60.0	39.1
Kansas	1 692.3	969.0	723.3	2 775.5	1 143.1	1 632.4	57.3	41.2
Kentucky	2 079.1	1 560.4	518.8	3 479.5	1 986.2	1 493.2	75.0	57.1
Louisiana	2 494.0	1 718.7	775.4	4 733.5	2 294.1	2 439.4	68.9	48.5
Maine	714.1	468.5	245.6	1 214.9	578.4	636.6	65.6	47.6
Maryland	3 691.8	2 127.7	1 564.1	6 013.0	2 112.8	3 900.2	57.6	35.1
Massachusetts	5 792.8	2 934.3	2 858.5	7 968.4	3 394.9	4 573.5	50.7	42.6
Michigan	8 016.8	4 843.7	3 173.1	12 687.3	4 800.9	7 886.5	60.4	37.8
Minnesota	3 601.7	2 485.6	1 116.2	5 803.2	2 023.7	3 779.5	69.0	34.9
Mississippi	1 260.1	969.3	290.9	2 431.6	1 135.4	1 296.2	76.9	46.7
Missouri	2 923.5	1 598.1	1 325.4	4 523.6	1 740.8	2 782.7	54.7	38.5
Montana.......	582.7	312.4	270.3	1 072.3	498.4	573.9	53.6	46.5
Nebraska	1 208.1	612.9	595.1	1 799.1	680.1	1 119.0	50.7	37.8
Nevada	564.8	329.1	235.7	930.4	353.4	577.0	58.3	38.0
New Hampshire	525.0	200.2	324.8	947.9	454.9	493.0	38.1	48.0
New Jersey.....	6 826.6	3 103.7	3 722.9	9 722.8	3 423.8	6 299.0	45.5	35.2
New Mexico ...	743.2	597.6	145.6	1 400.3	653.6	736.7	80.4	47.4
New York......	22 444.8	10 743.2	11 701.5	32 177.9	8 175.2	24 002.7	47.9	25.4
North Carolina .	3 275.2	2 384.8	890.4	5 426.0	2 148.3	3 277.7	72.8	39.6
North Dakota ..	445.1	296.3	148.8	854.3	465.5	388.8	66.5	54.5
Ohio	6 856.6	3 570.8	3 285.8	11 871.5	3 943.7	7 927.8	52.1	33.2
Oklahoma	1 681.8	1 139.0	542.8	2 937.0	1 400.4	1 536.5	67.7	47.7
Oregon	1 884.5	973.1	911.3	3 359.7	1 396.8	1 962.9	51.6	41.6
Pennsylvania ...	9 074.6	5 590.8	3 483.7	13 746.5	6 180.7	7 565.8	61.6	45.0
Rhode Island ...	741.3	438.8	302.4	1 199.7	641.5	558.2	59.2	53.5
South Carolina .	1 578.6	1 187.6	391.1	2 814.3	1 559.7	1 254.6	75.2	55.4
South Dakota ..	433.6	200.1	233.5	813.3	429.6	383.8	46.1	52.8
Tennessee	2 425.0	1 529.5	895.5	4 266.1	1 833.3	2 432.8	63.1	43.0
Texas	8 178.3	4 750.1	3 428.2	12 873.1	5 133.2	7 739.9	58.1	39.9
Utah	827.0	531.3	295.7	1 523.0	750.9	772.1	64.2	49.3
Vermont	391.3	229.8	161.5	618.0	374.5	243.4	58.7	60.6
Virginia........	3 468.1	2 053.8	1 414.3	5 671.8	2 456.3	3 215.5	59.2	43.3
Washington	3 004.0	2 100.0	904.0	4 963.9	2 267.5	2 696.3	69.9	45.7
West Virginia...	1 157.1	903.4	253.6	2 013.6	1 129.2	884.4	78.1	56.1
Wisconsin......	4 048.3	2 733.3	1 315.0	6 147.0	2 088.7	4 058.3	67.5	34.0
Wyoming	401.3	233.3	168.0	638.3	283.7	354.7	58.1	44.4

SOURCE: Bureau of the Census, *Governmental Finances in 1976-77*, U.S. Department of Commerce, Washington, D.C. 1978.

sage of Proposition 13. Public finance experts point out that a high degree of "local fiscal strain" will be reflected, in the long run, by the outmigration of businesses and households. At the extreme, proponents of the "Laffer curve" argue that many states and local jurisdictions are already taxed to such an extent that they could increase revenues by reducing tax rates.

Our measures of fiscal conditions are primitive. Commentators focus upon such readily available measures as taxes paid per capita or per $1000 of personal income. These measures ignore several facts. Some states are able to export a substantial portion of their tax burdens.[3] Others have extensive local manufacturing and commercial activity and so residents need pay only a low tax rate. States also differ in their need for social services. A state with relatively large and young families will face high per capita education costs. A large share of poor and elderly will raise a state's health costs. Thus some states can provide high quality public services at low tax rates, while others must impose high taxes and suffer inferior services.

A true comparison of state fiscal conditions would be based upon a comparison of both revenue sources and expenditure demand factors. Unfortunately, while the conceptual model for this type of analysis has been laid out (Barro, 1978), the necessary empirical work has yet to be performed. We can only provide conceptual discussion.

Revenue Base

States gain revenue from their own revenue base and external aid from the federal government. A state's revenue base is a measure of the total resources it can draw upon to raise public revenues. It includes the income and wealth of residents, and non-residents who may work in the area, sales by business, business property, corporate income, and mineral rights. Total revenue is simply revenue base multiplied by fiscal effort. State fiscal capacity is a measure of the revenues that can be raised from a state's own sources. Personal income is the simplest measure, since it is related to the ability to pay. It is used by some federal grant programs, such as General Revenue Sharing, that attempt to redistribute from rich to poor jurisdictions. But income is inadequate as a measure for several reasons: (1) it does not reflect personal wealth —holdings of both financial and non-financial assets; (2) it does not reflect business income and assets; (3) it ignores interstate spillovers;[4] and (4) it ignores price differences among states that may reduce money income differences.

Expenditure Demand Factors

A given level of per capita revenues does not support the same level of per capita services in each state. Demands for state services are determined by four factors:

1. *Demographic Characteristics.* States with large numbers of dependent people—children, the elderly and the poor—will have to spend more per capita than other states to provide equal levels of services to those in need. Also, interstate differences in demand-related factors, such as population density, climate, terrain, and age of the public capital stock, will lead to different expenditure needs.

2. *Costs.* Industrial and highly urbanized states face higher prices for goods, services and wages than other states, and thus will have to spend more per capita to achieve a given level of services.

3. *Scope of Responsibility.* The greater the responsibility of the state relative to local governments and the broader the eligibility for program participation, the more the state will have to pay per capita to support those services.

4. *Other Factors.* Inherited obligations—pensions, mandated programs such as air and water pollution abatement, and services to non-residents—will all lead to interstate differences in expenditures need.

Taken together, per capita needs provide a picture of local fiscal conditions. Although a full analysis of this sort has not been completed, several partial studies have been performed.

One approach has been to develop a weighted measure of the tax base for interstate comparisons. States are compared by the amount of revenue they could raise if they applied an average (of all states) tax rate to each component of their tax base.[5] Recently, the Advisory Commission on Intergovernmental Relations has computed the fiscal capacity of states during 1964-1975 using this method. They were able to characterize both the present level and the current direction of recent trends in local fiscal capacities.

States were ranked both on their "pressure" in 1975, expressed as their own source taxes as a percentage of "adjusted income" (U.S. state median - 100), and on the annual average percent rate of change in adjusted tax effort, 1964-1975 (U.S. state median - 100) (Table 5 and Figure 2). New York, for example, at 171 over 537, had a tax effort 71 percent above that of the median state, and this effort had grown more than five times faster than the median state since 1964.

Summing up these findings, the Advisory Commission noted that rates of change in fiscal pressure are far from uniform, and some states, such as New York and Massachusetts, are now under relatively extreme pressure. As a result, it is certainly much easier to make a case for federal aid for central cities (New York and Boston) located in states already under extreme fiscal pressure than for central cities, such as St. Louis and Cleveland, located in low pressure states. In general, the Northeast and Midwest are experiencing rising fiscal

pressure, while the Sunbelt states are in the falling pressure category.

Table 5
A Two-Dimensional Measure of Relative State-Local Fiscal Pressure Using the Representative Tax Method to Estimate Fiscal Capacity: Dividing the States Into Quadrants: 1964-75
(Indexed on Median)

High and Falling		High and Rising	
Hawaii	130[1]/ 99[2]	New York	171/537
Wisconsin	126/ 29	Massachusetts	146/381
Vermont	119/ 20	California	132/310
Washington	109/ 95	Minnesota	127/173
Utah	103/ 65	Rhode Island	124/281
North Dakota	102/ -3	Maryland	121/347
Indiana	101/ 98	Michigan	118/241
		Maine	114/143
		New Jersey	113/324
		Pennsylvania	112/244
		Illinois	111/362
		Arizona	108/102
		West Virginia	106/242
		Mississippi	106/163
		Connecticut	106/149
		Virginia	102/396
		District of Columbia	101/419
		Delaware	101/377

Low and Falling		Low and Rising	
Colorado	100/-37	South Carolina	99/169
Iowa	99/-16	New Mexico	98/105
Oregon	98/ 66	Kentucky	96/205
Louisiana	98/ 62	Ohio	95/196
South Dakota	97/-94	Missouri	94/186
Kansas	96/-18	Nebraska	88/195
North Carolina	94/ 76	Wyoming	86/130
Idaho	94/ 12		
Montana	93/ 4		
Georgia	92/ 92		
Alabama	90/ 71		
Tennessee	89/ 14		
Nevada	86/100		
Alaska	88/-95		
Texas	84/ 41		
Florida	80/ 24		
Arkansas	79/ 68		
Oklahoma	79/ -3		
New Hampshire	79/-27		

[1]Fiscal pressure for 1975.   [2]The index of change is from 1964-75.

SOURCE: Advisory Commission on Intergovernmental Relations, *Measuring the Fiscal Blood Pressure of the States*, M-111, Washington, D.C. February 1977.

Figure 2
A Two-Dimensional Measure of Relative State-Local Fiscal Pressure Using the Representative Tax Method to Estimate Fiscal Capacity: State-Local Systems More than One Standard Deviation from the Median: 1964-1975

SOURCE: Same as Table 5.

However, regional location is not always an accurate predictor. Even in the Northeast and Midwest, state and local policymakers have been able to alter significantly the size and composition of their public sectors—compare the fiscal pressure of Vermont and New Hampshire, Michigan and Ohio. This diversity, ACIR concluded, makes it difficult to obtain widespread agreement about either the severity of the problem or the best way to resolve it.

The ACIR methodology is not without its critics. Akin (1973) argues that the concept of a "national average tax rate" is misleading, and instead relates per capita revenues to the whole array of tax bases through regression analysis. However, the ACIR analysis does show that states differ in their local fiscal efforts. Although differences in effort are not necessarily an indication of anything amiss, such large and rapidly growing differentials have left the "high and rising" states with little padding in the face of economic slowdowns that reduce their tax base and require increased expenditures.

CONSTRAINTS ON STATE FISCAL POLICY: IGNORANCE

Fiscal policy debates invariably circle around the question of incidence—who pays and how much? For those anxious for a definitive answer, we must conclude that few tax questions have received as much attention, and as little resolution, as tax incidence. Further, we believe that future academic research on the subject of incidence is unlikely to provide information that is truly useful for state and local policy makers. Two hundred years ago, Edward Gibbon observed that all taxes must eventually fall on agriculture, and his insight remains one of the surest in judging who pays for taxes. *The less the mobility of a factor of production, the greater the share of the tax burden that factor bears.* The most important implication of this fact is that it matters whether we are discussing tax incidence from the national or local perspective,[6] and in the long run or the short run.

From a national perspective, few factors are mobile. Thus the burden of the property tax, on average, falls on capital. But from the local perspective, capital and some segments of the labor force are mobile—they can move to another city or to the suburbs—and, therefore, the burden of interjurisdictional differences in taxes falls on land and relatively immobile low income labor. In a high taxing area, land prices are bid down, and consumer product prices driven up, relative to lower taxing areas. A local grocery store cannot move out of town and maintain its customers, so it must pass on part of the tax burden in terms of higher prices if it is to stay in business. Local households who cannot easily find employment elsewhere must shoulder the extra costs.

Similarly, factors are much less mobile in the short run than in the *43* long run. If a state increases corporate income taxes, a firm will not immediately leave. If it competes in the national market with many other firms, it cannot raise its prices. In the long run, it can move, expand activity in out-of-state branches, and gradually reduce its ongoing tax costs, although it will have suffered a capital loss on the value of the site it owns. Office firms that lease space will not even suffer this loss. There will be a tendency, therefore, for landowners in high taxing locales to experience a decline in property values relative to those elsewhere. The process will apply to industrial, commercial and residential property in the long run.

To summarize, inter area variations in property tax rates are borne by landowners, local consumers and immobile capital. The average national property tax burden is borne by capital.

Similar considerations apply to personal income taxes. Skilled and relatively affluent households operating in a national market require compensation for taxes in the form of higher wages, shifting the burden onto business, consumers and landowners. The burden thus falls onto less mobile segments of the labor force.

Another point is that the overall impact of fiscal actions depends not only on who pays the taxes but also on who benefits from the services for which the taxes pay. A state which used the receipts from a progressive tax system to pay for roads and parks in high income areas and a subsidized local opera would be less progressive in overall incidence than a state which spent the revenues generated by a similar tax system on social services for the poor. The difficulty in tracking the incidence of public expenditures has precluded such a broad based study. In fact, there are no overall studies of the incidence of expenditures on a comparative basis, although a few studies have examined the incidence of particular expenditure programs.

The results of the complex operation of the tax system is that incidence studies are rendered almost impossible. In fact, trying to ascertain who pays how much is not a fruitful exercise for state agencies. We should instead try to understand the direction of the impacts—how local taxes affect household and business migration, for example—rather than calculate the dollar burden.

CONCLUSIONS

Before beginning our analysis of the efficiency, equity, and administrative convenience of alternative business and personal taxes, three general observations should be stressed. The first point that must be made, and it will, regrettably, be repeated throughout this paper, is that there is a great deal that we do not know about the impact of taxation.

Second, it is difficult to arrive at any universal prescription concerning tax policy. A tax that is relatively efficient and equitable in one place may be inefficient and inequitable elsewhere. The impacts of a tax depend heavily upon the local economic and social structure—the type of businesses, prevailing wages, energy costs, local labor skills, transportation linkages, and so forth.

Finally, we should note that it is difficult to "prove" that one tax is superior to another, not only because evidence is inconclusive and local factors must be taken into account, but also because the application of our criteria does not lead to unambiguous conclusions. Tax A may score higher on some criteria, and worse on others, than Tax B. Which is chosen depends upon the importance attached to each criterion. The primary purpose of this discussion is to assess· how taxes perform relative to each criterion in order to allow for a more informed local choice. Specific recommendations, based upon the author's judgment, are a purely secondary purpose.

FOOTNOTES TO CHAPTER 3

1. *Robinson v. Cahill* in New Jersey; *Horton v. Meskill* in Connecticut; and *Levittown Board of Education v. the State of New York.*

2. This discussion rests upon the excellent recent analysis by Barro (1978).

3. A state may export a part of its tax load by taxing firms that sell their products in other states, by taxing the extraction of minerals, or by taxing tourist-related industries, providing it enjoys some monopoly power.

4. Commuters from New Jersey that work in New York City form a part of New York's tax base. But the District of Columbia—another area with a substantial number of "out-of-state" commuters—is constitutionally proscribed from directly taxing commuters.

5. See ACIR (1971 and 1977) and Mandel (1971).

6. This point is argued by McLure (1977) in an important article reconciling the two views of property tax incidence, the "old" view that it falls on land and consumers, and the "new" view that it falls on capital.

WHAT SHOULD STATES DO ABOUT STATE/LOCAL FISCAL RELATIONS?

The division of fiscal responsibility among the federal, state and local governments has been compared to a layer cake, with each layer relying on a different tax and responsible for different functions. This structure is failing to address effectively the development problems that beset many states and local areas. This chapter analyzes what steps can be taken to improve the structure.

Since World War II, the federal government has relied primarily upon income taxes, state governments have relied upon sales taxes, and local government have used property taxes. However, this neat division has buckled in the face of rapid growth in both federal and local expenditures.

States still rely primarily on sales taxes—both general sales taxes, and selective taxes on such items as gasoline, liquor, and cigarettes. However, the postwar growth in revenue has stemmed largely from the expansion of state personal income taxes, which grew from only 7.4 percent of total revenues in 1948 to 21 percent in 1977 (Table 6).

States differ widely in their revenue systems.[1] There are also wide differences among states in the taxes that local government units are allowed to levy. While the property tax still predominates, twenty-six states now allow local sales taxes, and eleven allow local income and payroll taxes. The latter are either levied at a flat rate on all earned income originating in the jurisdiction,[2] or at a flat rate on all earned and unearned income.[3] A third type of local income tax is a graduated income tax on earned and unearned income, authorized by the state of New York and enacted by New York City in 1966.

In some states, local taxes are collected as supplements to state taxes. Local supplements to state taxes have three essential characteristics: they are optional; they are administered by a state agency; and the tax base is uniformly defined for all jurisdictions. Two states, Indiana and Maryland, have authorized local supplements to their income taxes.[4]

Table 6
Share of Total State Tax Revenue of Selected State Taxes,
1922, 1948, 1977

Type of Tax	Percentage of State General Revenue from Own Sources		
	1922	1948	1977
Sales and Gross Receipts	14.1	59.9	43.2
General	-	21.9	25.4
Selective	14.1	38.0	17.8
Motor Fuel	1.4	18.7	7.5
Tobacco	-	5.0	2.9
Other	12.8	8.0	7.4
Income	10.7	16.1	28.6
Individual	4.5	7.4	21.0
Corporate	6.1	8.7	7.6
License	31.5	14.5	3.8
Other*	43.7	9.6	24.4

*Includes fees and charges.

SOURCE: James A. Maxwell and J. Richard Aronson, *Financing State and Local Governments,* The Brookings Institution, Washington, D.C., 1977, p. 42; and Bureau of the Census, *Government Finances in 1976-77,* U.S. Department of Commerce, Washington, D.C., 1978.

WHAT'S WRONG WITH THE PRESENT SYSTEM?

The present structure of state/local fiscal relations contains several problems:

■ First, the system is inequitable. Poor jurisdictions face growing service demands but inadequate reserves. State aid is not effectively redistributive.

■ Second, local reliance on the highly visible and politically unpopular property tax will have to be reduced over time. Court decisions concerning school financing are likely to hasten this process.

■ Third, there is growing resentment against paying for redistributive public services and grants through local taxes.

■ Fourth, local jurisdictions have come to rely upon a massive increase in federal funds to survive the mid-1970s recession. This aid is unlikely to continue. States will have to assume increased fiscal responsibility for local jurisdictions.

■ Finally, the exemption of certain classes of property from property taxes places a heavy burden on occupants of non-exempt property. **47**

Table 7
Equity Characteristics of State Fiscal Policy

State	Income Redistribution Power[1] of the State — Local Tax System						Fiscal Equalizing Power of[4] State Expenditure Programs			Coalition of American Public[6] Employees Equity Ranking					
	Incidence Classification[2]			State and Local Tax Burden, Family Income		Tax[3] Redist. Index	P.C. State Equal. Outlays	Outlays as a % of Personal Income		Sales Tax	Pers. Income Tax	Bus. Tax	Prop. Tax	Gen. Tax Admin.	Overall Rank
	Prog.	Prop.	Reg.	$10,000	$50,000			Percent	Index[5]						
Alabama			X	8.2	6.4	78	183.59	4.0	111	47	40	51	48	35	51
Alaska		—	X	N.A.	N.A.	—	859.05	9.0	259	13	8	19	25	20	10
Arizona			X	7.7	6.9	89	233.03	4.4	122	7	38	11	21	35	22
Arkansas		X		7.0	7.4	106	76.67	1.7	47	21	19	24	40	13	27
California		X		8.8	10.8	123	126.37	2.7	75	44	3	2	8	1	4
Colorado	X			9.5	8.4	88	189.06	3.2	89	9	21	19	28	6	8
Connecticut	X			12.3	7.6	62	122.58	1.8	50	51	43	31	32	20	35
Delaware		X		8.3	8.6	104	421.33	6.5	181	13	4	31	43	46	29
D.C.	—			N.A.	N.A.	—	—	—	—	28	15	11	17	32	17
Florida			X	4.9	2.6	53	209.65	3.8	106	25	43	38	5	35	33
Georgia		X		7.8	8.0	103	181.10	3.6	100	31	20	11	2	27	13
Hawaii	—			N.A.	N.A.	N.A.	491.49	7.4	265	3	10	28	22	18	7
Idaho	X			7.8	9.0	115	170.18	3.3	92	4	11	3	45	17	6
Illinois		X		10.7	7.6	71	273.68	4.0	111	49	37	40	14	27	42
Indiana		X		9.6	6.8	71	141.72	2.5	69	29	42	38	27	35	44
Iowa		X		12.1	9.5	79	208.28	3.5	97	10	26	11	7	46	16
Kansas		X		10.5	8.5	81	169.28	2.8	78	27	23	40	34	20	31
Kentucky		X		9.0	7.7	86	171.24	3.5	97	42	34	50	9	35	43
Louisiana		X		4.6	3.6	78	247.01	5.1	142	8	41	40	51	35	46
Maine			X	9.7	7.8	80	215.59	4.5	125	36	5	11	11	20	8
Maryland	X			12.8	11.7	91	158.09	2.5	69	34	29	35	5	11	23
Massachusetts		X		13.9	11.6	83	291.64	4.8	133	4	16	8	40	20	11

State														
Michigan	X		8.8	8.7	99	257.23	5.0							
Minnesota	X		12.1	11.8	98	260.34	4.5	125	12	2	19	15	18	5
Mississippi	X	X	6.6	4.5	68	178.95	4.4	122	48	27	40	46	46	50
Missouri		X	9.3	7.9	85	140.89	2.6	72	39	33	35	35	20	39
Montana	X		9.2	8.8	96	225.48	4.2	117	13	36	4	50	5	20
Nebraska	X	X	9.0	7.4	82	88.95	1.5	42	4	13	31	29	13	12
Nevada	X	X	5.5	3.1	56	134.65	3.0	83	32	43	40	25	13	34
New Hampshire	X	X	8.2	5.1	62	70.70	1.3	36	13	43	26	15	43	30
New Jersey		X	14.4	9.6	67	147.70	2.2	61	20	35	28	20	13	26
New Mexico	X		7.4	7.6	103	273.21	5.7	158	1	9	45	33	20	20
New York	X		10.6	15.0	142	337.46	5.2	144	24	6	26	18	32	19
North Carolina	X		9.0	8.8	98	209.94	4.3	119	32	17	6	9	34	15
North Dakota	X	X	7.8	8.5	109	161.16	2.7	75	19	28	8	43	6	18
Ohio	X	X	7.9	7.1	89	146.08	2.5	69	26	31	8	23	43	28
Oklahoma	X		6.4	6.8	106	129.91	2.5	69	11	18	45	39	46	37
Oregon	X		8.4	10.6	126	118.99	2.1	58	13	14	4	1	6	1
Pennsylvania	X	X	11.5	8.9	77	248.32	4.2	117	40	39	28	23	27	35
Rhode Island	X	X	10.5	8.8	84	269.85	4.7	131	43	21	31	31	46	45
South Carolina		X	7.3	8.0	109	83.45	1.8	50	45	24	31	36	27	40
South Dakota	X	X	8.8	5.2	59	102.92	2.1	58	22	43	35	12	2	23
Tennessee	X	X	7.2	4.0	56	142.67	3.0	83	50	43	18	42	31	48
Texas	X	X	6.1	3.5	57	174.69	3.1	86	38	43	47	46	6	47
Utah	X	X	8.2	7.4	90	177.64	3.7	103	35	32	1	37	10	25
Vermont	X	X	10.4	11.0	106	187.64	3.8	64	2	12	24	12	43	14
Virginia		X	7.9	7.5	95	151.02	2.6	72	36	25	19	30	35	32
Washington	X	X	6.8	3.5	51	268.21	4.0	111	46	43	49	19	2	37
West Virginia	X	X	5.6	6.1	91	169.09	3.4	94	41	30	11	38	46	41
Wisconsin	X	X	14.8	14.6	99	269.24	4.8	133	18	1	19	3	11	3
Wyoming		X	5.8	3.3	57	135.95	2.2	61	23	43	47	49	35	49

NA means not computed by ACIR

SOURCES: Coalition of American Public Employees, *Tax Equity in the 50 States*, Washington, D.C., February 1979; Advisory Commission on Intergovernmental Relations, Staff Calculations.

NOTES:
1. The power of the State/Local tax system to redistribute resources from the rich to the poor through taxes.

2. Classified as Progressive (Prog.), Proportional (Prop.) or Regressive (Reg.) by the ACIR, based on the tax redistribution index: states with an index value of less than 90 are classified regressive, 90-110 proportional, and greater than 110, progressive.

3. The index is defined as the tax burden for a family of four in the $50,000 class as a percent of the burden for a family of four in the $10,000 income class. Median state index is 87.

4. State expenditure programs that reduce interjurisdictional economic and fiscal disparities are listed in John Shannon's testimony before the Senate Committee on Governmental Affairs, June 28, 1978.

5. The index expresses the state's equalization expenditure as a percent of the state median.

6. The ranking shows the ordering of the equity of each tax by state, with the most equitable being 1, and so on.

The clearest expression of the strains in the system have been the pleas for direct federal aid by some cities, and the taxpayers' revolt. More subtle, and more harmful, has been the tendency for high income households to move into homogeneous suburban communities to avoid paying for—and living near—poor and minority groups.

EQUITY   The present system does not ensure either vertical or horizontal equity. Vertical inequity arises because state taxes are often regressive—that is, the higher a household's income, the lower the share of income paid in taxes. Table 7 shows the burden of state and local taxes as a percent of household income for families earning $10,000 and $50,000. New York has the most progressive system, as well as one of the highest rates. A family earning $10,000 would pay 10.6 percent of its income in taxes, one earning $50,000 would pay 15.0 percent. By comparison, the comparable rates in the state of Washington are 6.8 percent and 3.5 percent (this issue is discussed in more detail in Chapter 7). Only New York, Idaho, Oregon and California have progressive systems.

Horizontal inequity arises because households with similar incomes living in different jurisdictions pay different tax rates for similar public services. Those living in jurisdictions with high concentrations of low income households will tend to pay much higher tax rates to finance locally-funded redistributive services. States can reduce horizontal inequity by assuming fuller fiscal responsibility for services for the needy, by targetting expenditures toward poor jurisdictions, by instituting state revenue sharing, or by state tax sharing programs. The inadequacy of present efforts has been recognized in court decisions that call for greater state efforts to equalize education expenditures among jurisdictions.

The urban crisis has brought the question of horizontal equity to the foreground. Many of the distressed cities in the Northeast face appalling tax burdens because of extensive social programs and receive relatively little assistance from their state governments. In many instances, the fact that the city tends to be run by a Democratic government while the statehouse is dominated by Republicans has further contributed to political polarization.

A recent study by the Coalition of American Public Employees ranked states according to the equity of their taxes. Their rankings, shown in Table 7, were based on the extent to which a state's taxes placed burdens on the poor, or gave relief to corporations, and the steps states took to make individual taxes less regressive—such as the exemption of food from sales taxes. Oregon emerges as having the most equitable system, Alabama the least.

The Advisory Commission on Intergovernmental Relations (Shannon, 1978) has ranked states according to the extent to which their expenditure patterns reduce interjurisdictional fiscal disparities. A state payment was classified as equalizing if it involved:

■ Direct or indirect public welfare expenditures;
■ Direct or indirect medicaid expenditures; or
■ State expenditures based on local needs such as schools, urban aid, and revenue sharing.

ACIR found that states scoring highest are those characterized by centralized fiscal systems (Alaska, Delaware, Hawaii, and New Mexico) and those with high welfare obligations (Massachusetts, New York, and Rhode Island). Their index of the fiscal equalizing power of state expenditures is shown in Table 7. States have greatly expanded their redistributive programs, both through grants to local governments and through direct expenditures. Intergovernmental transfers totaled $57 billion in FY1976, but when direct state expenditures for state-local functions are added, the sum climbs to $73 billion. This compares with only $21 billion in FY1965. The comparable figures for federal assistance are $1.2 billion and $21.0 billion (National Governors' Association, 1978a).

($ Billions of State Assistance to Local Governments)

Period	Total	Local Schools	Highways	Public Welfare	Health & Hospitals	General Local Support	Other State Aid to Local Govt.
1964-65	$20.9	8.7	5.7	2.3	2.6	1.1	0.5
1975-76	$72.8	29.6	11.6	12.2	9.7	5.7	4.1

A number of states have undertaken a form of state revenue sharing—grants allocated to jurisdictions in much the same way as federal revenue sharing. Allocation should ideally be from richer jurisdictions to poorer ones. Unfortunately, this rarely occurs. First, like federal revenue sharing, population is used in the allocation formula which spreads funds among all jurisdictions. Second, many of the state taxes earmarked for redistribution are regressive—collecting proportionately more per capita from poor jurisdictions than rich ones. Collection and redistribution according to population makes poor jurisdictions worse off. State revenue sharing programs are summarized in Table 8. Only Florida has an explicitly equalizing factor as an important element in its allocation formula, but the regressivity of the excise tax vitiates its effect (Rafuse, 1974).

Twenty-six states share receipts from one or more taxes with their local governments. In 1973, these payments amounted to less than 13 percent of the total non-categorical aid payments to local governments **51** in those states (ACIR, 1974). This policy offers little opportunity for redistributing funds from rich to poor jurisdictions.

Some states have taken steps to increase aid to localities. North Dakota adopted a statutory sharing of 5 percent of the state's income tax revenue in November 1978. Starting in 1979, Kansas will distribute 3.5 percent of its sales tax revenues among its cities and counties, 65 percent of which will be based on population and 35 percent on the value of local property. This replaces the sharing of cigarette and liquor taxes. Massachusetts has assumed full fiscal responsibility for local court costs ($88 million), and has distributed over $200 million to distressed local communities. Connecticut is compensating local governments for tax losses attributable to incentive tax abatements. Michigan and California have devised aid programs for distressed areas. New York now pays for all SSI costs. California and Maryland have assumed county medicaid costs and Iowa pays the full administrative costs for the food stamp program.

While these are positive steps, there are still many states that are not doing enough to redress local fiscal imbalances. The reluctance of many states to assist the economically disadvantaged has given rise to the view that income redistribution is primarily the responsibility of the federal government, and the role of state and local governments is marginal.

Growing Opposition to Local Property Taxes

Recent referenda have provided taxpayers with a means of protesting rising tax levels to all elected officials. While all taxes have been growing, property tax increases have been the most visible. They have risen as a result of inflation, rising property values, and reassessment.[5] The fiscal squeeze during the 1974-75 recession increased the enthusiasm of local assessors for reassessment. Gallup reports that 58 percent of survey respondents felt their property taxes had increased "a great deal," while only 36 percent felt that federal income tax increases fell into this category; 25 percent named state and local income taxes, and 15 percent the sales tax.

As well as through increased rates and assessed valuations, the burden of the property tax has been increased through the dramatic decline in the number of taxpayers itemizing their federal tax returns. In 1969, more than 60 percent of all returns were itemized, allowing households to deduct local taxes when computing taxable income—a savings, on the average, of 30 percent of the cost of local taxes. By 1978, as a result of the increase in the standard deduction, only 25 percent of the nation's households were itemizing. In nine years, the share of households paying the full cost of local taxes has nearly doubled.

52 The group that has felt this additional bite most strongly are middle

Table 8
State Programs of Revenue Sharing with Local Governments, $25 Million or More: Characteristics and Relative Degree of Fiscal Capacity Localization Achieved, 1973

State	Source of Revenue	Allocation Factors	Amount Shared (millions)	Relative Degree of Equalization
Arizona	General sales tax	Counties: origin basis Municipalities: population	$83.8	Negligible
California	Motor vehicle licenses	Population	245.0	Negative
	Cigarette taxes	Sales tax collections and (cities) population	74.3	Negative
Florida	Miscellaneous excise taxes	Population, sales tax collections and (inversely) property tax capacity	171.3	Slight
Illinois	Personal and corporate income taxes	Population	95.0	Slight
Louisiana	Tobacco taxes	Population	26.0	Negative
	General funds	Population and number of homesteads	86.0	Negligible
Michigan	General sales tax	Population	116.0	Negligible
	Personal income tax	Population and relative tax effort	82.0	Negligible
	Intangibles tax	Population and relative tax effort	27.5	Slight
Minnesota	General sales tax	Population	100.7	Negligible
New Jersey	General sales tax	Population	25.0	Negligible
New York	Personal income tax	Population, personal income, real property full value	450.8	Slight
North Carolina	Intangible property tax	Population, origin, property tax rates	25.6	Negligible
Ohio	Miscellaneous taxes	Population, municipal valuation, "need)	117.7	Negligible
Tennessee	General sales tax	Population	27.5	Negligible
Wisconsin	Miscellaneous taxes	Population, property tax rates, value of utility property	265.4	Negligible

SOURCE: Advisory Commission on Intergovernmental Relations, *Federal-State-Local Finances: Significant Features of Fiscal Federalism,* Report M-79 (1974), pp. 79-81. Interpretation by Rafuse, 1974.

income taxpayers—the same group that has probably tipped the political balance in favor of tax limitations.

Taxpayers, angry about spiralling property taxes, have a hard time knowing who to blame—the assessor, the school board, the city council, or the county board. But much of the blame must be borne by the inequity of the tax itself. Real estate, the only real asset for low- and moderate-income households, is but a small share of the assets of the relatively affluent. Yet property taxes are usually limited to real estate,[6] making the tax relatively regressive. Assessment practices are far from satisfactory in many areas. Because assessments fail to keep up with market trends, housing in growing areas pays a lower rate than housing in declining areas. Property owners are often unaware of what their taxes will be until they receive a notice. Assessors have been accused of political favoritism. Publicity about low taxes paid by prominent local politicians has not endeared the assessment system to taxpayers. And finally, taxes are paid in lump sums, rather than through the more subtle weekly payroll deductions used for income taxes.

Resistance to Income Redistribution at the Local Level

Many of those objecting to taxes are especially incensed by the cost of welfare and other social services that are essentially redistributive.[7] There are two somewhat differing themes running through this protest. First, some object to what they feel is waste—"welfare cheats." Others object to the unequal sharing of the burden of providing services to the poor.

Expenditures on transfer payments and social services for the needy have risen dramatically, and federal grants have only partly offset the cost. Transfer payments now constitute 13 percent of national income, compared with 10 per cent a decade ago. In spite of a spate of welfare reform rhetoric during the last two presidential election campaigns, little has been done to make the delivery of services and income transfers to the poor more efficient. The recession of 1974-75 served to swell the welfare rolls and increase medicaid payments.

More troublesome than the overall level of the costs of these redistributive services is the unevenness of the burden among states and counties. Residents of Northern states and of the large metropolitan areas in those states face a much heavier burden than those elsewhere. New York City government spent $338 per capita on welfare in FY 1974, of which 75 per cent was covered by state and federal grants. Detroit only spent $2.63 per capita in the same year. A move across county or state lines may bring about a significant reduction in taxes levied to pay for welfare. This inequity—the feeling that neighbors may not be paying their share—has led to a desire to restrict local

54

Table 9
Percent of State Personal Income Collected As State Income Tax
and Disbursed as State-Local Welfare Expenditures, FY 1975
(States Above Median Welfare Spending)

State	Percentage of State Personal Income:	
	Collected as State Income Tax	Disbursed as State-Local Welfare Payments From Own Funds
District of Columbia	3.35	2.66
Massachusetts	3.75	2.16
Michigan	2.00	1.61
California	2.94	1.59
Rhode Island	2.32	1.58
New York	4.08	1.53
Hawaii	3.91	1.41
Pennsylvania	2.47	1.34
Wisconsin	4.29	1.29
Minnesota	4.72	1.25
Vermont	3.05	1.19
New Hampshire	0.87	1.13
Maine	1.35	1.12
New Jersey	0.54	1.09
Illinois	2.08	1.08
Ohio	2.06	1.02
Oregon	4.33	1.02
Iowa	2.81	0.92
Kentucky	2.45	0.90
Delaware	4.29	0.90
Maryland	3.11	0.88
Connecticut	0.77	0.82
Washington	0.00	0.81
Alaska	4.38	0.77
Colorado	2.45	0.77
Median for 50 states	2.50	0.75

SOURCE: John Shannon, Testimony before House Committee on Banking, Currency and Housing, September 28, 1976, reprinted by the Committee in *The Rebirth of the American City*, U.S. House of Representatives, Washington, D.C., 1976, and U.S. Bureau of the Census, *Governmental Finances, 1974-75, Washington, D.C. 1976.*

taxes so that the burden is passed on to a higher level of government. Ultimately, many taxpayers would like to see federal assumption of welfare responsibility, following the example of the Supplemental Security Income program (SSI).

Table 9 shows the percentage of state personal income collected through state income taxes and the percentage disbursed in state and local welfare payments for selected states with high personal income tax rates. High income tax payments are associated with a high level of locally financed welfare payments.

The Prospect for Future Federal Aid

The rapid expansion of federal aid to cities and states in response to the sharp 1974-75 national recession enabled most areas to escape relatively unscathed.

This cornucopia is unlikely to continue. In fact, Richard Nathan of the Brookings Institution has pointed out that the most generous period for fiscally distressed areas is likely to have been the period immediately preceding the announcement of President Carter's urban program. Among the several casualties of a conservative Congress, Antirecessionary Revenue Sharing was not renewed before Congress adjourned in December 1978. Local Public Works will not be extended, and the soft public works program has been abandoned.

Tax Exempt Property

Between one-third and one-half of all real property is exempt from property taxes— worth between $800 and $1000 billion (Hellman and Sifniotis, 1977; and Netzer, 1973). Seventy percent of the exempt property belongs to the federal, state or local governments, 15 percent is owned by religious groups, and the remainder belongs to schools, cemeteries, museums, and various charitable organizations. Central cities typically have the greatest concentration of exempt property. Yet exempt property requires fire and police protection, and its occupants must use roads, sewers, and water supplies. Owners of non-exempt property must pay extra. Compensation by higher levels of government has been less than adequate in most states.

State Mandated Programs

One final problem with state/local relations is the issue of state mandated programs whose cost must be borne, in whole or in part, by local governments. Many of these mandates involve programs that local governments wish to carry out anyway, and provide strictly local benefits. The most commonly mandated functions are: solid waste disposal standards; special education programs; workmen's compensation for local personnel; and local public sector pension provisions (ACIR, 1978c).

56

Mandates that may seriously affect local fiscal conditions include those that set quality standards for local public service delivery, those that set tax assessment and collection procedures, those that influence the definition of the local tax base (excluding certain property from the property tax base, for example) and those that set local public employee salary or benefit levels.

There are no estimates of the cost of mandates to local governments by state. A survey by the Advisory Commission on Intergovernmental Relations found that New York, California, Minnesota and Wisconsin had the most state mandates, while the least were in Southern states, particularly Alabama. Opponents of mandates claim that they represent a loss of local autonomy, allow state legislators to introduce programs without any idea of their true cost, and create local fiscal distress. Proponents argue that mandates are necessitated by poor local administration, and ensure that services are coordinated and uniform throughout the state. Three states have constitutionally limited the state's mandating powers (Alaska, Louisiana, and Pennsylvania), ten have provisions for state reimbursement to local areas for the costs of mandated programs, and 25 states require mandates to be accompanied by notes indicating their fiscal impact.

WHAT CAN BE DONE TO IMPROVE THE STATE/LOCAL FISCAL SYSTEM?

Improving the horizontal and vertical equity of the present system and providing local fiscal relief in the face of federal cutbacks will require extensive reforms. The most important steps that state governments can take are:

■ Facilitate metropolitan revenue and tax base sharing.
■ Target the allocation of state aid and expenditures much more effectively.
■ Develop state-financed property tax circuit breakers.
■ Increase the progressivity (or reduce the regressivity) of the state tax structure.
■ Reimburse local governments for the cost of state mandated programs.
■ Lobby for increased federal funding of programs aimed at the poor.

Metropolitan Revenue and Tax Base Sharing The sharp disparity between the economic characteristics of suburban and central city residents has contributed to urban fiscal problems. The incidence of poverty in suburbs is below 8 percent, but over 15 percent in central cities. Per capita suburban incomes are more than 10 percent above central city incomes. As we shall see in Chapter 7, this outcome is not accidental; it has been **57** caused, in part, by the heavy redistributive tax burden in central cities. Yet many suburban dwellers commute downtown, implicitly taking advantage of the public services provided by the central jurisdiction.

This has led several observers to recommend policies that would, in Peterson's (1976) words, "reunite the city with its market area." These policies range from sharing part of the proceeds of taxes within a metropolitan area to allowing cities to tax commuters or annex their suburban communities.

Progress in each of these areas has been slow and the prospects for swift action are not bright.[8] But the situation is not hopeless. In 1978, a voter-elected regional council was approved in Portland, Oregon. The body will coordinate programs throughout the metropolitan area, and may assume responsibility for the provision of public services. The metropolitan area of Portland, however, is not as racially or economically segregated as those of more fiscally distressed areas where tax sharing and regional government are even more necessary. Most state governments have shown reluctance to take the necessary steps in the face of strong suburban opposition. Retargeting state grants, while politically more expedient, does not remove the underlying incentives that perpetuate interjurisdictional segmentation. Peterson (1978) observes that "only tax changes that go beyond the city's borders and produce tax-base sharing at the metropolitan or state-wide level promise significant reduction in the magnitude of the overall city tax burden." Revenue sharing is a much less equitable and effective method of reform, for it fails to equalize fiscal effort across jurisdictions (Fischel, 1976).

The federal government can assist states in the difficult task of implementing tax base sharing. As Barro (1978) argues, "there are many ways in which incentives for structural change could be built into the various federal grant programs." The Comprehensive Employment and Training Act was the first to take steps in this direction by providing a small bonus to jurisdictions that formed consortia.

Although unpopular in suburban areas, tax base sharing is a necessary step in placing state/local fiscal relations on a more equitable basis.

Targeting State Expenditures

The basic principle in attempting to improve interjurisdictional horizontal equity is that the state must take from rich jurisdictions and give to poor ones, or from rich households and give to poor ones. That is, targeting must be improved both in grants to local jurisdictions and in grants to individuals.

Any allocation formula for a jurisdictional grant that includes population as an argument is bound to be almost useless. Similarly, **58** any matching fund system will probably fail because poorer jurisdictions are frequently unable to come up with the necessary match. Unfortunately, state politics makes effective targeting difficult. A narrowly targeted program tends to be spread further and further over time as political pressure broadens jurisdictional eligibility.[9]

The circuit breakers discussed below are one example of a program that does target effectively and automatically. Perhaps the most important reform will have to be in the area of state education and assistance. At present, in some states, rich school districts actually receive more per pupil than poor districts because of matching fund requirements.

Even if there were no political constraints on how to distribute state assistance, there would still be many technical problems in designing an efficient and equitable allocation formula. Consider the problem of education aid. How are we to take account of the following issues:

■ The number of pupils per capita differs among school districts.
■ The share of students requiring special training and facilities differs among districts.
■ Some districts have a high per capita amount of commercial and industrial property to provide revenue.
■ Per pupil income and wealth differ among districts.
■ The amount of necessary maintenance and repair on facilities differs among districts.

This is not the place to solve such vexing grant allocation questions. But it is the place to make the point that state involvement in re-distributive programs will increase in the future, and the combination of political and judicial pressures will necessitate the development of effective allocation formulas.

State-Financed Circuit Breakers[10]

The circuit breaker is a form of property tax relief in which benefits depend on both household income and on the amount of property taxes paid. The circuit breaker may take two forms (ACIR, 1975):

> Under the threshold approach, an "acceptable" tax burden is defined as some fixed percentage of household income (different percentages may be set for different income levels), and any tax above this portion of income is "excessive" and qualified for relief. Under the sliding scale approach, no threshold is defined. Rather, a fixed percentage of property tax . . . is rebated for each eligible taxpayer within a given income class; the rebate percentage declines as income rises.

Wisconsin (1964) was the first state to provide property tax relief this way. By 1970, six states had circuit breakers, and by 1978, 29 states **59**

Table 10
Summary of State
Revenue Sharing Receipts and Circuit Breakers

State	Residential Property Tax Per Capita 1975	State Revenue Sharing Receipts FY 1977 Per Capita	State Revenue Sharing Receipts FY 1977 $ Millions	Circuit Breaker, 1977 Total Program Cost ($ Millions)	Circuit Breaker, 1977 Number of Beneficiaries	Circuit Breaker, 1977 Cost Per Beneficiary
Alabama	22	9.67	35.7	—	—	—
Alaska	79	10.89	4.4	—	—	—
Arizona	106	11.25	25.9	NA	NA	NA
Arkansas	35	10.85	23.3	0.7	8,916	75.76
California	202	10.61	232.4	85.0	440,000	193.18
Colorado	97	9.22	24.2	11.0	58,875	187.00
Connecticut	199	9.09	28.3	24.7	101,574	243.70
Delaware	53	11.95	7.0	—	—	—
D.C.	102	—	—	0.6	6,000	100.00
Florida	82	7.94	67.1	—	—	—
Georgia	72	9.16	46.3	—	—	—
Hawaii	86	11.25	10.1	4.2	NA	NA
Idaho	51	9.55	8.2	4.0	17,323	231.00
Illinois	117	9.96	112.0	100.0	405,000	250.00
Indiana	88	8.62	46.0	0.8	28,665	29.45
Iowa	87	9.48	27.3	9.6	83,200	114.56
Kansas	83	8.49	19.7	8.8	62,955	140.17
Kentucky	37	10.81	37.4	—	—	—
Louisiana	32	11.96	46.9	—	—	—
Maine	104	12.63	13.6	4.3	20,786	209.10
Maryland	126	11.82	48.9	20.8	83,863	248.12
Massachusetts	229	11.78	68.1	—	—	—
Michigan	130	10.00	91.3	275.6	1,234,800	223.18
Minnesota	103	11.85	47.1	134.2	857,277	156.54
Mississippi	38	14.02	33.5	—	—	—
Missouri	76	8.64	41.5	7.0	56,260	124.57
Montana	95	10.65	8.1	—	—	—
Nebraska	91	8.95	14.0	—	—	—
Nevada	133	8.43	5.3	1.4	10,560	127.84
New Hampshire	163	8.54	7.3	—	—	—
New Jersey	216	9.37	68.7	—	—	—
New Mexico	34	12.09	14.4	1.5	40,000	37.50
New York	181	16.38	293.7	NA	NA	NA
North Carolina	48	10.92	60.3	—	—	—
North Dakota	54	9.38	6.1	1.2	9,964	120.20
Ohio	86	8.28	88.6	44.6	329,462	135.42
Oklahoma	41	8.58	24.1	0.4	4,159	85.93
Oregon	128	9.99	23.8	74.1	502,575	147.52
Pennsylvania	62	9.81	115.6	58.9	413,974	142.32
Rhode Island	150	13.12	12.3	0.01	249	51.92
South Carolina	42	11.81	34.0	—	—	—
South Dakota	80	10.78	7.4	1.5	15,095	98.51
Tennessee	52	9.47	40.7	—	—	—
Texas	68	8.61	110.6	—	—	—
Utah	65	9.80	12.4	0.9	10,000	95.00
Vermont	137	12.87	6.2	7.7	36,516	210.05
Virginia	83	8.63	44.3	—	—	—
Washington	123	11.22	41.1	—	—	—
West Virginia	39	12.54	23.3	0.02	1.265	13.94
Wisconsin	115	11.55	53.7	48.1	234,201	205.55
Wyoming	66	8.70	3.5	—	—	—

NA means not available.

SOURCE: ACIR, *Family Tax Burdens Compared Among States and Cities,* Washington, D.C., 1978; John Shannon, "After Jarvis: Tough Questions for Fiscal Policy Makers," *Intergovernmental Perspective,* Summer, 1978; U.S. Bureau of the Census, *Governmental Finances 1976-77,* Washington, D.C., 1978; "Tax Wealth on Fifty States," *State Government News,* July 1978.

and the District of Columbia had adopted some form of circuit breaker. Most states without circuit breakers have below average property tax rates.[11]

In 1977, more than 5 million households received circuit breaker benefits totalling nearly $1 billion—an average of nearly $184 per household (Table 10). Both homeowners and renters are covered in 24 of the states.[12] Benefits vary among states, from $250 per beneficiary in Illinois to $14 in West Virginia.

Since the purpose of a circuit breaker is redistributive, its design must ensure that the greater benefits flow to those in greatest need, and that no benefits are received by those not in need. To ensure that the program operates effectively, one must resolve such issues as *eligibility* and the *distribution of benefits* among the eligible.

Three of the most common characteristics used to define eligibility are income (in all but four states), age and occupation. Upper income limits range from $3,750 for single homeowners in New Mexico to no limit for elderly homeowners in the District of Columbia. Some upper limit seems essential. Some programs are limited to the elderly because many elderly are poor, tend to be relatively immobile, live on fixed incomes, and cannot easily adapt to soaring local property taxes. However, this may make the program relatively regressive since there are also many relatively affluent elderly. An upper limit of about $12,500 seems reasonable.

Treatment of renters is a difficult problem. Most programs include renters, but homeowners receive more generous benefits (ACIR 1973a). Programs that extend benefits to renters assume that an average of 20 percent of the rent reflects local property taxes, but the range is from only 6 percent in New Mexico to 30 percent in Illinois. There is also a problem in that incomes in the two groups are not directly comparable. A homeowner is "better off" in some sense than a household with a comparable money income that rents because of the tax advantages. Whether this should be taken into account depends upon whether the circuit breaker is used primarily as property tax relief or as an income supplement. As an income supplement, a circuit breaker can never perform as well as a cash transfer, but may be more politically expedient and administratively simple. Overall, the circuit breaker works well in targeting benefits to those who need them.

To reduce interjurisdictional movement by households seeking maximum benefits, responsibility for financing a circuit breaker should rest with the state government, not with local jurisdictions. The program would, in effect, redistribute resources toward jurisdictions with relatively high concentrations of low income households.

The cost of a circuit breaker depends on the percent of the "excess" property tax a household receives in a rebate. This is defined by two factors: the percent of income that tax payments cannot exceed for *61* threshold type programs, and the design of the sliding scale. In 1970, ACIR (1973a) estimated that if 7 percent of income were the threshold level, a nationwide program would cost $2 billion and reach 13.5 million households. A 5 percent threshold would cost $4.3 billion, reaching 21 million households; and a 4 percent threshold $6.1 billion, reaching half of all households. If costs have risen proportionately with property tax payments—surely a conservative estimate—costs today would be more than double. Within states, net benefits would be greatest in those jurisdictions with a high incidence of poverty and high property tax rates.

While central cities have greater concentrations of the poor, they have lower valued housing and, often, lower property tax rates. In general, a circuit breaker would tend to provide greater per capita benefits for cities than suburbs, depending upon the fraction of rent ascribed to property taxes—the higher the proportion of rent, the greater the "urban" benefit of the program. The benefits would be effectively targeted toward poorer jurisdictions, allowing them to raise local taxes without imposing extreme hardship upon the local poor and lower middle income groups. It would, therefore, strengthen the fiscal position of those jurisdictions with a relatively weak fiscal base. It would also weaken property tax limitation movements, and, perhaps, avoid too many repetitions of the clumsy efforts made in California.

The program does target effectively on distressed cities. Table 11 shows 15 cities grouped according to their urban conditions index, showing the per capita residential property tax and the percent of the population below the poverty level—the two main determinants of the relative benefits under a circuit breaker program. The final column shows a crude index of the likely relative benefits under a circuit breaker—calculated as the product of their tax payments and poverty rates indexed to the average of all 15 cities. Among the severely distressed cities, only Buffalo scores significantly below 100, because of its relatively low poverty rate.

The state-financed circuit breaker may encourage increased activism by the poor, since they would not have to bear the cost of increased local services. It might also encourage their concentration in the central city. This seems unlikely since a considerable fraction of the poor already receive some form of housing assistance, and they are concentrated in central cities already.

A more important problem is that the burden of assisting the poor through a state-financed circuit breaker will be much heavier in high-taxing states with high concentrations of the poor. Given the generally accepted proposition that the poor are a federal rather than a local responsibility, a strong argument could be made for federal help. However, increased federal expenditures for local tax relief seems

62

Table 11
Urban Conditions Index,
Per Capita Residential Property Tax,
Percent Poverty, and Benefit Index
(Selected Cities)

City	Urban Conditions Index[a]	Per Capita Residential Property Tax, 1976	Percent Poverty 1970	Index of Per Capita Benefit from Circuit Breaker (15 City Average = 100)[b]
St. Louis	351	228	33.6	148
Newark	321	493	22.1	211
Buffalo	292	307	14.8	88
Cleveland	291	286	17.0	94
Boston	257	483	15.3	143
Unweighted Average	302	359	20.6	137
Baltimore	226	196	18.0	68
Philadelphia	216	237	20.8	95
Detroit	201	352	14.7	96
Chicago	201	319	14.3	88
Atlanta	118	256	19.8	98
Unweighted Average	192	272	17.5	89
Denver	106	284	11.5	63
Los Angeles	74	419	11.2	91
Dallas	39	247	13.3	64
Houston	37	286	13.9	77
Phoenix	20	218	11.6	49
Unweighted Average	55	290	12.3	69
All 15 Cities	183	307	16.8	100

SOURCES: Paul R. Dommel et al., *Decentralizing Community Development,* The Brookings Institution, Washington, D.C., January 1978; *Monthly Tax Features,* The Tax Foundation, August 1978.

[a] For definition see Dommel et al., 1978.

[b] Calculated as:

$$\frac{\text{Per Capita Residential Property Tax}}{\text{Mean for all 15 Cities (= \$307)}} \quad X \quad \frac{\text{Percent Poverty}}{\text{Mean for all 15 cities (= 16.8)}}$$

unlikely at the moment. One possible source of funds for circuit breaker assistance is the state portion of revenue sharing funds.

The fraction of revenue sharing grants going to states could be used to help pay for state initiated property tax relief, with some increased federal grants used to reward states that have already introduced equitable circuit breaker programs. Table 10 shows state revenue sharing receipts in both total volume and per capita terms in FY 1977. States could use their $2.5 billion in revenue sharing grants to help pay for circuit breaker. States would not be compelled to participate. Circuit breakers would also deflate local "Proposition 13-type" movements.

Increased Tax Progressivity

The redistribution from rich to poor jurisdictions can be influenced not only through state expenditure patterns but also through state revenue practices. There are several ways that states with regressive tax collection systems could do this:

■ Those poor states with rich endowments of natural resources can raise severance taxes to export their tax load.
■ Sales taxes can be modified to include special allowances for clothes, food and utility payments (Chapter 7).
■ Circuit breakers can be provided for the poor.
■ States without personal income taxes can switch from regressive sales taxes to progressive income taxes.
■ States with flat rate income taxes, which are regressive because of the offset against federal income taxes, could consider introducing a graduated income tax.

Some states[13] have flat rate rather than graduated taxes. There are four arguments in favor of switching to a graduated income tax (Moscovitch, 1972):

1. Graduated taxes are more equitable since they require the well-to-do to pay a higher share of their income than the poor. In fact, since higher income taxpayers tend to submit itemized federal tax forms, a flat rate state tax results in the poor, who do not itemize, paying a higher share of their income in state taxes than the rich.
2. A graduated tax allows the state to shift a large part of the local tax burden onto the federal government.
3. The graduated tax is more responsive to changes in income—such income taxes rise more than proportionately.
4. State tax revenues can be increased without increasing the tax
64 burden on the poor.

For example, for FY 1973, for the state of Massachusetts, it was calculated that a move to a graduated structure from the actual flat rate with no change in total revenue could have yielded the following range in incidence (Moscovitch, 1972):

Tax Bracket in 1973	1973 Tax Structure		Shift to Progressive Tax*	
	Actual Tax Paid	Net Cost After Federal Tax Deduction	Actual Tax Paid	Net Cost After Federal Tax Deduction
$ 5,300 - $ 6,600	153	153	38	38
$ 9,300 - $10,600	292	292	111	111
$13,000 - $20,000	588	459	390	304
$26,000 - $33,000	1367	930	1705	1159
$100,000	5451	2453	11,723	5275

*Based upon the New York State graduated tax structure modified to yield unchanged total revenue for Massachusetts.

Such a change would have reduced taxes for 1.3 million households, raised them for 95,000, and reduced the federal tax liabilities of Massachusetts residents by $100 million.

It has long been believed that a progressive tax is more stabilizing. The theory is that as incomes fall during a recession, progressive taxes fall more than proportionately, softening the blow, leading expenditures to fall less than they would otherwise. Some evidence suggests that, since the burden of a recession does not fall equally on all groups, the shift from a graduated to a progressive tax would have little stabilizing impact (Cassidy, 1970).

However, as we argue in Chapter 7, states that try to increase the progressivity of their income taxes in absence of similar changes in neighboring states may find their affluent households leaving, thus raising the burden on the less well-to-do who remain. A federal grant system that rewarded states with progressive forms of taxation would help to soften this blow.

State Reimbursement of Mandated Program Costs

There are several options for states that wish to reduce the inequities arising from state mandated programs. First, states may be required to pay, in full, for mandated program costs. Florida now requires full state reimbursement for any state general law that requires local jurisdictions to spend additional funds or that changes local tax assessments or authoriza- **65** tions. Tennessee, Hawaii, and Michigan enacted state reimbursement measures on proposed new mandates as part of their constitutional amendments for spending limits in 1978. This may not necessarily contribute to fiscal equalization. It depends on the distribution of the benefits of the mandated program. An alternative is to place constitutional limits on the types of programs that can be state mandated. This is a relatively clumsy recourse. Finally, states may require that each mandate be accompanied with detailed estimates of its fiscal impact. This will ensure that program costs are an integral part of the mandate debate.

The principle of reimbursement can be extended to cover compensation to local authorities for tax exempt state facilities. Over 50 percent of Boston's real property tax base is tax exempt, representing an annual revenue loss of $100 million. In 1978, New Jersey enacted a law requiring state reimbursement for tax losses due to state-held properties. Connecticut has a law requiring state compensation for losses due to the tax exempt status of hospitals and universities. Not only should other states follow these leads, they should also lobby the federal government for an effective compensation program for federal property.

Increased Federal Assistance[14]

In may seem futile to call for increased federal assistance at a time when federal programs are being cut back. However, the emphasis should be on improved targeting of assistance rather than on increasing the level. One way to reduce the interstate inequities that arise as a result of the concentration of the poor in certain areas would be through federal assumption of the responsibility for programs currently financed, in part, at the local level. The clearest candidates are welfare and health programs.

Federalization of Welfare. In 1974, the Supplemental Security Income program (SSI), encompassing state-run programs for the disabled, blind, and aged, was federalized. However, this was not a pure case of federal assumption, since states must supplement federal benefits so that no one who received assistance under the superceded programs suffers a reduction in benefits. States may also voluntarily supplement federal benefits, and most have chosen to do so.

Welfare federalization proposals focus primarily on the AFDC program, which is the largest welfare program, spending $9.2 billion in 1975, of which 56 percent was financed by the federal government, 37 percent by the states, and 7 percent by local governments (Hamilton and Rabinowitz, forthcoming). But federalization would not save states their $4 billion. Most proposals call for a nationally uniform schedule and eligibility standards, with provision for state supplementation, very much on the model of SSI. No proposal would maintain the present differences in benefits, for that would imply a massive federal subsidy flowing North from the low-benefit Southern states. With high federal benefit levels, the incentive for high-benefit states to supplement would be small, and they would therefore gain substantial fiscal relief. With low federal levels, these states would receive little additional assistance from federalization. A relatively low level seems the most likely outcome from any successful reform.

Local fiscal relief would depend on state decisions about the division of the total fiscal relief between states and local jurisdictions. Full federal assumption would provide substantial relief to only six major cities—Baltimore, Denver, New York, Philadelphia, San Francisco, and Washington, D.C.—to a few smaller cities, and to a few urban counties in New York and California (Hamilton and Rabinovitz, forthcoming). However, these gains would be diluted if state governments cut back aid to localities, imposed the supplementation costs on the cities, or reduced the taxing authority of the city to a degree commensurate with the reduction in welfare costs.

Rather than complete federal assumption, John Shannon (1976 b) has suggested a "welfare payments circuit breaker." Under this program, the federal government would provide grants to those states in which state and locally-financed welfare payments claimed a share of state personal income that was above the national average. Thus, in 1975, the average state spent 0.75 percent of total personal income on state and locally-financed welfare (Chapter 7). In Massachusetts, the fraction was 2.16 percent. Those overburdened states would receive a federal grant equal to some percentage of their overburden— perhaps 50 percent, or $240 million in the case of Massachusetts. The program has the advantage of helping heavily burdened states without some of the problems of full federal assumption.

Federalization of Health Care Programs. National health care financing may provide as much state and local fiscal relief as welfare federalization. Table 12 shows that state and local governments spend more for health and hospitals (when medicaid is counted as a public welfare program), net of federal assistance, than they do on welfare. If a comprehensive health care system could assume medicaid costs and medicaid is included in the health category, then state and local spending for welfare (excluding medicaid), net of federal aid, was slightly over $7 billion in 1975, compared with over $22 billion for health (including medicaid). A broad national health program has considerable potential for local fiscal relief.

States differ in their per capita outlays for health services, ranging from less than $2 per capita in Arizona, Indiana, Maine, Maryland, Nevada, North Dakota, Oregon, and Wyoming, to $97 per capita in New York, $52 in California, and $50 in Pennsylvania (1975 data reported in Hamilton and Rabinovitz). The fiscal relief from federal- **67**

Table 12
**State and Local Spending and Federal Aid for Public Welfare
and Health and Hospitals, 1974-75**
($ Billions)

Function	State and Local General Expenditure	Federal Aid to State and Local Governments	State and Local Expenditure Net of Federal Aid
Public Welfare (including Medicaid)	27.2	14.4	12.8
Health and Hospitals	18.8	2.1	16.7
Medicaid	12.6	6.9	5.7
Public Welfare (less Medicaid)	14.6	7.5	7.1
Health and Hospitals (including Medicaid)	31.4	9.0	22.4

SOURCE: All data except Medicaid from U.S. Bureau of the Census, *Governmental Finances in 1974-75,* GF75, No. 5, Washington, D.C., September 1976, Table 6. Medicaid data from Hamilton and Rabinovitz (forthcoming).

ization would be enjoyed primarily by a few large urbanized states.
   Other Possibilities for Federal Assumption. There are other functional areas in which the federal financial role could become substantially larger. Education is the most obvious candidate. The federal government could take on a much larger fraction of the burden of financing elementary and secondary education. State-local spending for public schools is currently so large that a federal assumption of even a small fraction of this burden (special education, for example) would have a significant effect on the finances of the whole state-local sector. Higher education also offers the opportunity of either an expanded federal program of tuition aid or an expansion of institutional grants to colleges and universities—both of which would reduce state costs. Other possibilities include expanded federal support for both the construction and operation of mass transit or for capital construction projects. Federal involvement would take the form of larger grants.

FOOTNOTES TO CHAPTER 4

1. Details of state business and household taxes are given in Chapter 5 and 7 respectively.

2. These taxes are authorized in five states: Alabama, Kentucky, Missouri, Ohio, and Pennsylvania.

3. Authorized by the state of Michigan, 1964. The enabling legislation mandates a one percent tax on residents and 0.5 percent tax on non-residents. No other state has yet followed Michigan's lead.

4. In Maryland, every county, and Baltimore city, is required a levy a supplement of at least 20 percent of the state liability, and may adopt a rate as high as 50 percent. Indiana authorized local supplements in 1973 and one-third of all counties and 315 small municipalities have enacted supplements.

5. The *Wall Street Journal* reported annual tax increases as high as 200 percent in parts of Southern California, 300 percent in Cook County, Illinois, and 126 percent in Bucks County, Pennsylvania ("Soaring Property Taxes Infuriate Homeowners," *Wall Street Journal,* 9/7/77.)

6. In some states, such as Virginia, there are taxes on the value of other assets, including automobiles, boats and furniture. However, this is unusual.

7. Asked in a Gallup Poll whether their community spent too much or too little on a number of local services, 42 percent of the respondents felt too much was spent on social services, and only 19 percent felt too little was spent. For all other services, more respondents felt too little was spent than too much ("The Big Tax Revolt," *Newsweek,* 6/18/78).

8. See ACIR, 1973b; Bahl and Puryear, 1976; Bahl and Vogt, 1975; and Peterson, 1976. See also the discussion of the issue in *Rebirth of the American City,* Volume 2, Committee on Banking, Currency and Housing, U.S. House of Representatives, Washington, D.C., 1976, p. 727ff.

9. A good example of the way that a program can be spread further and more thinly over time is the Community Development Block Grant program. Originally concentrated in a relatively few, poor communities, funds have been gradually extended to more and more urban communities by city governments.

10. This discussion has benefited from a manuscript by Steven Gold, *Property Tax Relief,* forthcoming.

11. The four major exceptions are Massachusetts, New Jersey, Nebraska, and New Hampshire.

12. Robert Reinhold, "Carter Weighs Pushing States to Assist Cities," *New York Times,* 2/12/78.

13. Illinois, Indiana, Michigan, Massachusetts, and Pennsylvania.

14. This discussion rests heavily on the excellent exposition by Barro, 1978, p. 94ff.

5

WHAT SHOULD STATES DO ABOUT BUSINESS TAXES?

Few policy discussions are fueled by as much passion, encompass as many conflicting parties, and are based on as little evidence, as the debate on what to do about business taxes. Households and consumers, who have borne the brunt of spiralling taxes, demand that the burden be shifted to businesses. Businesses, facing rising competition from the "New South" and the Far East, demand tax breaks. The unemployed demand jobs. And state governments need revenues. This chapter examines business taxes. The following chapter reviews the use of specific tax incentives to achieve state development goals.

There are several types of business taxes, and their use varies among states. The most important are:

■ *Business income taxes.* These include corporate, financial, and unincorporated business income taxes. Several states have no business income taxes,[1] but tax the value of output[2] or gross sales.[3] Revenues were $7.2 billion in FY 1976.

■ *Property Taxes.* These include taxes on the value of land and structures owned (or even leased) by the company. Some states and localities include the value of equipment and inventories when estimating property values. States collected $2.1 billion in property taxes in FY 1976, localities $32.9 billion.

■ *Payroll Taxes.* Companies must contribute toward unemployment insurance and workmens' compensation. These are not regarded as business taxes, nor are they regarded as being within the scope of state tax policy. They are computed on an actuarial basis and paid into a trust fund. Although they are not traditionally considered part of general state revenue, they vary among states and have an influence on development. Unemployment insurance premiums totalled $5.1 billion in FY 1976.

■ *Severance Taxes.* States with rich endowments of natural resources charge for each unit of raw materials extracted. For example, in 1978, half of Alaska's revenue from its own sources came from severance payments on oil production. In FY 1976, three quarters of all state severance taxes were accounted for by Texas ($800 million), Louisiana ($558 million), and Oklahoma ($151 million).

■ *Sales Taxes.* In some states, all sales, including interindustry purchases, are taxed; in most, only retail sales. General and selective

70

sales tax revenues account for nearly half of all state tax receipts.

■ *Excise Taxes.* Taxes on gasoline and fuel oil may be important to some companies. Rates exceed 10 cents a gallon in Connecticut, Hawaii, Michigan, New Hampshire, Rhode Island, Washington, West Virginia, and D.C. Recently, they were only 5 cents in Texas.

■ *License Fees.* States charge license fees to set up and operate businesses. Nationwide, these fees comprise 7.7 percent of state tax revenues, but they top 31 percent in Delaware, 16 percent in New Hampshire, and 15 percent in Nevada. General corporation license fees are collected in all 50 states, but Texas ($213 million), Pennsylvania ($200 million), and Michigan ($158 million) accounted for 50 percent of all such revenues in FY 1976.

This list is by no means exhaustive. States also have fees for motor vehicle registration, hotel room occupancy taxes, user fees for state services and facilities, water and sewer link-up charges . . . the list is limited only by the imagination of state finance departments over the last 200 years and the United States Constitution. The listed taxes do represent the major sources of revenue to state and local governments. Table 13 shows state revenue from the most important of these taxes.

Table 14 shows the characteristics of business taxes in each of the fifty states and the District of Columbia. Comparing business tax rates is extremely difficult. For example, although there is a wide range in corporate income tax rates, the actual differences in the burden may be very different from the data in the table. States differ in how they define the taxable income base upon which the rates are levied. For example, although the Colorado rate is half that of New York, the fact that New York reduces taxable income by an amount that is related to the amount of out-of-state sales, while Colorado does not necessarily do so (see below), reduces the differential. It is further reduced by the fact that New York does not include inventories in the property tax base, while Colorado does. Six states—Alabama, Arizona, Iowa, Missouri, North Dakota, and Utah—allow federal income tax payments to be deducted when calculating the local tax base. There are also great differences in special tax incentives (see following chapter).

A second point is that taxes influence business behavior not only through what is collected, but also through what is not collected. Through special tax treatment of certain types of activities—for example, accelerated depreciation of certain types of business equipment purchases—resources are diverted from other activities into the activity receiving special treatment. These "tax expenditures" are important. At the federal level, it has been estimated that tax expenditures—tax receipts foregone through special provisions—total over **71**

Table 13
State Revenue from Selected Business Taxes
FY 1977

Tax	Revenue ($ Millions)
Business property taxes (state & local)	32916.0
Corporate net income	7259.7
Licenses	6897.0
Severance	2028.7
Unemployment insurance (FY 1975)	5135.0
Motor vehicle fuel sales	8660.0

SOURCE: U.S. Bureau of the Census, *Governmental Finances 1976-77,* Washington, D.C., 1978, and data presented in Tables 14 and 22.

$100 billion. Yet there are no Congressional committees overseeing these large "programs." At the state level, even less is known. The only states which systematically prepare a thorough annual review of state and local tax expenditures are California, Wisconsin, and Maryland. Other states should follow suit.

With these caveats, we can still make some general observations (Table 14). There are large differences among states in unemployment compensation payments, expressed as a percent of total wages. These differences arise because of differences in local wage rates, benefit levels, turnover rates, and unemployment rates and duration. In Colorado and Texas, employer contributions average less than 0.2 percent of the total wage bill, but top 2 percent in Alaska and Rhode Island. Since wages are about one-third of total costs in manufacturing (two-thirds of value added), these variations will be much more important than the difference between corporate tax rates of 4 and 8 percent since corporate income rarely tops 10 percent of gross sales.

The discussion in this chapter yields several conclusions concerning the impact of business taxes:

■ First, contrary to popular belief, interstate variations in business income taxes have had little impact on the location and relocation of businesses. Firms have not fled South to escape from high corporate tax rates in the North. High rates may deter new investment—but not by a great deal.

■ Second, more important than *interstate* variations in business income taxes are *intrastate* variations in business property taxes. Business has expanded more rapidly in suburban or even exurban areas in part because of high taxes in central cities. Those same high taxes may have deterred investment and development. Some areas may benefit from shifting some of the tax burden onto land and off improvements.

■ Third, payroll taxes have exacerbated the problem of unemployment, and have probably affected low income employment.

■ Fourth, the corporate income tax is equitable inasmuch as it is related to ability to pay. However, it is not necessarily related to the value of services received, nor is it a predictable or stable revenue source. Some states may benefit by shifting toward a tax related to value added.

■ Fifth, the allocation of business income among states for multistate firms is inequitable. Some states have taken steps to reduce this inequity. Others should follow.

■ Finally, there is no reason for states to strive to cut business tax levels. In fact, households rather than business have paid for most of the increase in state expenditures since World War II. States with excessively high taxes may gain from reducing their disparities, and perhaps from simplifying their tax structure. But if taxes are to be cut, states should focus on personal rather than business taxes.

EFFICIENCY

Proponents of business tax cuts raise three efficiency arguments against the present level and structure of business taxes. First, they argue that high tax levels in some states deter business activities leading to reduced unemployment and lower investment. Second, interjurisdictional differences in tax rates have contributed to the movement of firms away from high taxing locales—particularly large central cities in the Northeast. Third, it is argued that business taxes fall on capital and therefore discourage new investment.

These beliefs are widely held. Their persuasive presentation by the business community has led to a general shifting of tax revenues from business to personal taxes, and to a general pressure on states to offer special tax incentives to stimulate investment and attract business. We shall see that there is no evidence to substantiate the first two claims, and that the third effect is relatively weak. However, in an area which has received little attention—payroll taxes—tax policy is contributing to unemployment among the unskilled.

Overall Tax Levels

Do high state taxes deter economic development? Few topics have been debated as heatedly and with less empirical foundation. Many state

Table 14
Characteristics of State/Local Business Taxes, 1977

State	Corporate Income Tax				Business Property Taxes		Other Taxes		
	Rate (%)[2]	Per Capita Revenue	UDI[6]	MSTC[7]	Inventories Exempt or Not Taxed	P.C. Business Property Taxes 1975	Unemployment Compensation as Percent of Total Wages (1976)	Licenses Per Capita	Severance Taxes Per Capita
Alabama	5.0	16.3	X	X		30.9	.53	24.5	3.1
Alaska	5.4 (+4.0*)	77.8	X	X		136.3	2.34	53.3	70.0
Arizona	2.5 - 10.5	20.2			X	127.3	.52	26.7	—
Arkansas	1 - 6	26.8	X	X	X	54.6	.85	29.4	4.2
California	9	58.6	X	X	X	171.3	1.34	23.6	0.1
Colorado	5	26.8			X	117.0	.19	25.9	1.7
Connecticut	10	46.4			X	152.6	1.35	29.1	—
Delaware	8.7	38.2			X	74.8	.87	186.8	—
D.C.	9.0[2]	—	X			94.8	—	—	—
Florida	5.0	21.3				80.6	.49	34.3	5.6
Georgia	6.0	26.5				90.4	.42	13.7	—
Hawaii	5.85 - 6.44	39.3	X	X	X	64.4	1.74	5.7	—
Idaho	6.5	35.3	X	X	X	109.2	1.14	46.3	0.4
Illinois	4.0	28.2	X			156.5	.42	35.7	—
Indiana	3.0[3]	16.1	X			143.5	.49	20.5	0.1
Iowa	6.0 - 10.0	26.8				175.9	.47	47.9	—
Kansas	4.5	40.3	X	X		170.0	1.01	30.2	0.3
Kentucky	4.0 - 5.8	38.5	X			57.9	.75	20.6	26.1
Louisiana	4.0 - 8.0	22.5				53.1	1.19	29.3	143.2
Maine	4.95 - 6.93	29.6	X		X	127.0	1.50	33.3	—
Maryland	7.0	26.7				86.6	.65	23.4	—
Massachusetts	8.33	56.1			X	201.5	1.69	14.0	—
Michigan	2.35	36.8	X	X	X	161.7	1.06	41.5	0.8
Minnesota	12.0	49.1			X	128.2	.80	34.5	14.6
Mississippi	3.0 - 4.0	17.1			X	59.2	.43	24.7	9.8
Missouri	5.0	14.0		X		107.9	.69	30.6	—
Montana	6.75	28.8	X	X		208.7	.95	32.1	39.1
Nebraska	4.0 - 4.4	17.8	X	X	X	189.8	.50	30.5	0.7
Nevada	—	—			X	120.4	1.60	74.3	0.2
New Hampshire	8.0	30.1			X	152.0	.93	36.9	0.1

State	Rate								
(row cut off at top)	5.0		X	X		61.5	.55	51.0	23.1
New York	10.0	63.3	X	X		187.7	1.17	23.1	—
North Carolina	6.0	28.5	X	X		69.7	.60	32.5	—
North Dakota	3.0 - 8.5	28.0	X	X		137.7	1.03	43.7	18.0
Ohio	-⁴	24.8				116.2	.55	39.3	0.4
Oklahoma	4.0	19.1	X	X	X	76.0	.55	43.5	54.0
Oregon	7.5	27.8	X	X	X	149.0	1.02	47.0	1.5
Pennsylvania	10.5⁵	52.3		X		101.3	1.16	50.3	—
Rhode Island	8.0	39.8	X	X	X	120.0	2.08	24.6	—
South Carolina	6.0	27.5	X	X	X	58.6	.53	17.1	0.4
South Dakota	—	2.9	X	X	X	186.6	.39	31.1	0.4
Tennessee	6.0	29.9				64.8	.72	40.8	0.4
Texas	—	—	X	X	X	123.5	.17	39.2	62.6
Utah	4.0	18.8	X	X		86.8	.83	18.6	9.0
Vermont	5.0 - 7.5	26.6	X		X	162.4	1.14	43.8	—
Virginia	6.0	25.6	X			74.5	.13	24.3	0.1
Washington	—	—				106.9	1.74	31.1	10.1
West Virginia	6.0	10.7	X			61.8	.51	25.5	—
Wisconsin	2.3 - 7.9	40.5			X	156.1	.87	28.1	0.1
Wyoming	—	—			X	217.2	.80	78.0	102.5

*Surcharge

SOURCE: Commerce Clearing House, *State Tax Guide 1978.* Chicago, Ill., 1978; Tax Foundation, *Facts and Figures on Government Finance,* Washington, D.C., 1977; U.S. Bureau of the Census, Governmental Finances, various years; estiamtes for the business property tax were made by subtracting per capita residential property taxes ("Tax Wealth in Fifty States," *State Government News,* July 1978), from total property tax revenues, per capita.

NOTES:

1. Where a range is given the state has a progressive corporate income tax. Highest and lowest rates are shown. Federal taxable income is used as a base except in Alabama, Arkansas, California, D.C., Louisiana, Minnesota, Mississippi, Oregon, South Carolina, Utah, and Wisconsin. Federal income tax paid is not deductible except in Alabama, Arizona, Iowa, Louisiana, Missouri and North Dakota.

2. A 10 percent surcharge is also imposed.

3. Domestic and interstate corporations pay a tax of 3 percent on adjusted gross income from sources in Indiana.

4. The greater of 4 percent of the first $25,000 of the value of stock plus 8 percent of the value over $25,000 or 5 mills times the value of each stock.

5. Do not allow the federal accelerated depreciation allowance in computing state taxable income.

6. Uniform Division of Income for Tax Purposes Act adoption is indicated by a check.

7. Multi-State Tax Compact membership is indicated by a check.

SOURCE: Will Meyers of ACIR.

NOTES:

a Membership subject to congressional approval (which hasn't come so far).

b UDI Act adopted only for allocation of nonbusiness income.

officials believe so, and have been persuaded by the demands from business that the tax burden be reduced.

The theory behind these demands is simple. If local taxes are lowered, then the local cost of doing business is reduced, existing firms become more competitive with firms elsewhere, and new firms may be induced to move in. The result is more jobs. This theory has achieved popular conceptualization in the "Laffer curve." Arthur Laffer, an economics professor at the University of Southern California, argues that if tax rates are increased beyond a certain point revenues decline because economic activity is reduced—labor force participation falls, investment is choked, and some businesses move to more favorable tax climes. There is no empirical evidence for the Laffer curve, although studies have found that rising personal income tax rates reduce male labor force participation, and rising business tax rates increase investment abroad.[4]

There is little evidence that overall tax levels are too high. A recent study by the Federal Reserve Bank of Boston found that the average U.S. business paid 4.4 percent of its income to state and local governments. In 1973, this broke down to 0.9 percent in corporate income taxes, 1.9 percent in property taxes, 0.8 percent in unemployment compensation contributions and 0.8 percent in "other business taxes."

The role of the corporate income tax and business property taxes on investment decisions has been small. Payroll taxes, which have received much less analytical and political attention, do appear to have raised the rate of unemployment and may have influenced industrial location decisions. Unemployment insurance premiums, workmen's compensation, and social security have raised the cost of labor, especially low wage labor, creating unemployment. They have raised the rate of layoffs and increased the duration of unemployment.

The level of unemployment insurance premiums has two effects in economic development. First, insurance checks allow workers to spend longer periods hunting for an attractive job before accepting a position (Ehrenberg and Oaxaca, 1976). The result has been an increase in the average duration of unemployment, and a tendency for the unemployed to seek higher paying employment. This is not necessarily bad, for the match between a worker's skills and preferences and his or her job will be improved, but it also means that the local *rate* of unemployment will be higher. In fact, the secular increase in unemployment—with strong cyclical variations—is due, in part, to the extension of unemployment insurance coverage to more sectors, the increase in the duration of assistance (through federal supplements to local programs), and increases in the level of assistance.

The second effect is upon the frequency of lay-offs. The amount that firms must pay in insurance premiums is meant to be linked to the frequency with which employees (or ex-employees) claim benefits.

However, there is an upper limit on the premium rate which is well below the "actuarial" rate, so that firms with a high labor turn-over are subsidized by less volatile companies. Feldstein (1976, p. 956) concludes that this subsidy "has a potentially very large impact on the rate of unemployment, causing layoffs when they would not otherwise happen and substantially magnifying the size of layoffs that do occur."

The states with a high concentration of their labor force in the volatile consumer durable industry will experience higher unemployment rates during recession as a result of the way the program is designed.

Interstate and Intrastate Tax Differences While the impact of tax levels has received little attention, the influence of interarea variations in the tax rates on growth and industry location has been studied extensively (albeit not satisfactorily). Do interstate differences in business tax levels affect industrial location decisions and spatial differences in economic growth? The answer, it seems, is very little. Counter to many myths, tax differences can be blamed for very few of the regional shifts in employment and for relatively few of the shifts from central cities to suburbs. *In fact, the major influence of taxes on economic development may not be through business taxes, but indirectly through personal taxes that influence the migration pattern of households and thus the growth of employment (see Chapter 7).*

There are several reasons for a conclusion that seems to contradict the conventional wisdom:

■ First, state and local tax payments are deductible for federal income tax purposes, and since corporate income is subject to a marginal federal tax rate of 48 percent, both the net burden and the amount of any differential are essentially cut in half.

■ Second, differences in tax rates are often compensated for by differences in the level and quality of local public services, which also affect business location decisions.

■ Third, the costs of many other factors vary among locations and may be much more important in location decisions. For most firms, labor costs are 20 times as large as state and local tax payments. A 2 percent wage differential is as important, therefore, as a 40 percent tax differential.

■ Fourth, local tax rate differentials are capitalized, at least in part, in property values. Land in a high taxing locale is depresed in value, while a low tax area will have higher land values.

■ Finally, there are relatively few footloose firms whose location decisions might be influenced by tax differentials.

One of the few studies that did find that taxes have a significant **77** effect was conducted for the Budget Bureau of New York City (Grieson et al., 1977). New York is in a somewhat unique position, since its commuters and businesses can move to either New Jersey or Connecticut and maintain close contact with the city. Both states have maintained a quite distinct tax structure—in part, one assumes, to try to syphon off some of the city's business. The study, which examined the shift from a gross sales tax to a corporate profits tax in 1966, concluded that manufacturing activity had left New York City in response to high taxes. In fact, a 10 percent increase in local taxes would reduce employment by about 3.5 percent. Unfortunately, it is difficult to identify what part of the ensuing exodus of manufacturing from the city is attributable to the tax change.

One reason why tax rate differentials within a metropolitan area have not contributed more to the suburbanization process is that part of the tax rate differential will be reflected in land prices. Land prices in a low taxing jurisdiction will, all other things being equal, be bid up when firms try to move in, while land in high taxing locales will decline in value. A firm must compare the tax savings with the higher purchase price of the site.

There is ample evidence of the capitalization of property tax differentials. There is also evidence that central city/suburban differences have not been very important. (Fuller and Towles, 1978; and Levin, 1976). However, as Cornia, Testa, and Stocker (1978) point out: "States do resort to fiscal and other incentives . . . These actions therefore suggest that these differences are not always fully capitalized in land prices. The capitalization process is limited by imperfections in the land market. Among these are a paucity of available sites or potential bidders, unique qualities of individual sites, and requirements of individual businesses, zoning and other land use restrictions, or limited knowledge of both sides of the market."

Thus the burden of high local taxes may be greater for firms with unique site requirements, which would tend to be large manufacturing concerns for whom rail spurs, harbor facilities and other features are important. Firms that are less mobile may, therefore, be induced to pay a higher tax rate than more mobile sectors. However, the few firms that fall into this category manage to gain a degree of political power that in the long run appears to minimize the extent to which local governments can capture any location rents.

The overwhelming evidence from many studies of industrial location decisions suggests that firms select their region on the basis of broad criteria, such as anticipated market growth, availability of raw materials, transportation, energy prices, and the quality of the labor force. The last factor includes the education and skills of the labor force, but also its wage rate and degree of unionization. Compared with these factors, state and local taxes shrink in importance.

Of course, irrefutable evidence is hard to find. It is difficult to determine why a company chooses a particular location. Rigorous econometric models rarely have appropriate or accurate data to work with, and questionnaires are only as reliable as their often biased respondents.

The near unanimity of findings from all sources gives some credibility to the basic proposition that tax rates have not been important. Schmenner (unpublished) concludes that "cities and towns need neither fear that high tax rates alone will drive out all industry nor rejoice that low tax rates guarantee rapid industrial development." Schmenner also points out that analyzing the relationship between taxes and location is confounded because the causation runs two ways. While industry may be marginally attracted by low tax rates, a heavy local concentration of industry can lead to a low tax rate because of the size of the base.

There are other aspects of the business tax structure that may also influence location decisions. From the point of view of computing taxable income, land cannot be treated as a depreciable asset. This encourages firms to avoid areas where land prices are high and may decline. The bias is toward suburban areas where prices are low and expected to rise. This bias is reinforced by the fact that capital gains are taxed at a lower rate than corporate income. This shelters rapid appreciation from taxes, encouraging location at the urban fringe. Fulton (1971, p. 10) illustrates this process with the case of a company that:

> 10 years ago acquired a very large site on Route 128 near Boston. Before the company could complete its plans for construction on the new site, it received—and accepted—an offer for a small portion of the property at what constituted a substantial profit. This was the first of many such transactions, all with increasing profitability, to the point where the company was realizing greater profits in land sales than in manufacturing. As a result, when another division of the same company planned expansion in the Chicago area, the company insisted on the acquisition of 100 acres, even though the utmost requirement for the proposed facility was only 10 acres.

Business Taxes and New Investment

The fact that the corporate income tax falls upon the net income from capital makes it quite progressive (see below) but also encourages the substitution of labor for capital, and discourages new investment. We do not know how powerful these tendencies are. Labor is also heavily taxed through such payroll taxes as unemployment insurance and social security. And capital receives a multitude of special allowances such as investment tax credits and depreciation allowances above the true depreciation rate.

Hodge (1979) studied the impacts of corporate income and business property taxes on investment across a sample of metropolitan areas. Although he found no significant influence as a result of the corporate income tax, investment was reduced in some industries by high property taxes. Comparing his results with others that found no influence on location, he hypothesized that "while the total profitability of location in one area versus another is not significantly affected by the presence of high property taxes, these taxes do affect the most profitable combination of inputs to be employed." This effect has not been strong.

Another inefficiency arises because the effective tax rate in manufacturing and commercial property is above that on residential property. This, coupled with more generous federal income tax allowances for residential investments (Peterson, 1978), has favored the residential sector. This has likely contributed to the suburbanization of the relatively affluent, and, therefore, to the social and fiscal problems of central cities.

EQUITY

Judging the equity of the business tax structure involves knowing the incidence of the taxes, and here there are many unanswered questions. Observers of state/local business taxes have alleged that the structure lacks both horizontal and vertical equity, and has been regressive inasmuch as households have borne an "excessive" share of the tax burden.

Horizontal Equity

The statewide corporation income tax ensures that it is relatively equitable, at least spatially. The wide variation in the business property tax is much less equitable, as we have seen. However, the way in which the net income tax base is defined—the inclusion of special allowances—does not guarantee intersectoral horizontal equity. The tax structure has not developed by chance. Rather, it reflects the needs of the most powerful local business sectors. For example, those industries that are relatively concentrated[5] in New York City—apparel, textiles, printing, leather, and miscellaneous manufacturing—are labor intensive and low profit. Yet taxes in New York City fall most heavily on high-profit, capital intensive firms (Gerard, 1974). This tendency for the tax structure to favor established local industries is fine while those industries are growing. But when these industries fall into decline, it could provide a barrier to local redevelopment by deterring expansion in less fiscally-favored but potentially growing industries. The long-established client relationship between older sectors and local politicians makes it difficult to adjust to new economic realities. In this case, the state, whose legislative process may be less centered

around specialized economic activities than that of the city government, could play an important function in neutralizing the local tax
bias. Again, New York provides a good illustration. The state investment tax credit reduces New York City's anti-capital intensive bias,
and thus encourages growth in non-traditional sectors.

Relation to
Public Services
There is no relation between the value of
public services used and the amount of
corporate income tax due. The property
tax is in some way related, since the more valuable the menu of public
services offered to a particular site, the greater the amount of property
taxes paid. But shifting across jurisdictional boundaries destroys
this simple relationship, and a firm in one jurisdiction may enjoy
greater services than a similar firm in another jurisdiction at a lower
tax "price."

Exporting Tax
Burdens Across
State Boundaries
Not all business tax revenues are paid by
state residents, either directly or indirectly. For a company with a nationwide market, consumers across the nation
pay part of the business taxes—the exact amount is determined by
the competitiveness of the industry and the particular advantages
the state offers for the industry in question. Basically, the more competitive the industry, the less the ability of the individual firm to pass
on local tax increases in the form of price increases. For example,
Alaska's taxes on oil extraction do nothing to influence the price that
is determined for oil in the world market. Louisiana and Texas can
influence the price and availability of natural gas elsewhere because
the price of domestically produced gas is below the world price. New
York can export some of its tax burden by taxing tourist-related
activities such as hotel occupancy—and Colorado can tax skiing—and
these taxes will be paid by the residents of other states.

The equity of tax exporting depends upon two vital factors: 1) Who
benefits from the local services paid for by the exported tax; and 2)
who, in other states, pays the tax. Thus one could argue that New York
City manages to export a tax burden on out-of-staters through its 4
percent sales tax surcharge on the state 4 percent rate because only the
rich will travel from out of state to take advantage of the city's unique
and high priced retail outlets. But the issue is less clear-cut. The sales
tax is, overall, regressive (see the following chapters). Taxing recreation and tourism may be progressive because high income households
tend to travel more extensively. But taxing raw material extraction
may not be—for example, low income households spend a higher proportion of their income on utility bills than do high income households. Politically, it is expedient to try to export a portion of the local **81**

tax burden. But there is no guarantee that this will improve equity.

One of the most difficult equity problems in developing state business tax policy rests with the computation of the taxable income of companies that operate in more than one state. Typically, the total taxable income of a company is "allocated" among the states in which the company operates according to three factors: the share of the company's sales, employment (or payroll), and plant and equipment within the state in question.[6] Each factor is weighted equally. Thus a company which has 75 percent of its employees and plant and 10 percent of its sales in a given state will pay taxes to that state on 52.8 percent of its taxable income.

The diversity of tax structures and tax base definitions has created an equity and administrative nightmare for multi-state firms. This leads to considerable inequity. From the viewpoint of the relationship between public services received and taxes paid, the share of employment and plant should be weighted much more heavily than sales, since the level of economic activity a much better measure of the use of local services (roads, transit use, fire protection, etc.). Horizontal equity is also impaired, because of two equally profitable and equal size companies, the one with the largest share of its sales out-of-state will pay the lowest tax.

In fact, the inclusion of sales in the formula creates an incentive for firms to move out of the state in which they make the majority of their sales. Consider a company that sells all of its output in state A, and that is able to move to state B, which has similar taxes and factor prices. It will reduce its tax burden by 33 percent by moving. Transportation costs will increase, and other factor prices may not be identical. But for a multibranch firm, there is a "tax incentive" to concentrate its employment expansion in branches in states where the firm's sales are relatively low.

Aware that firms in national markets can—quite inequitably—escape paying taxes in states where they only have sales, many states have either joined the Multi-State Tax Commission or adopted the Uniform Division of Income for Tax Purposes Act, which includes throwback provisions.[7] Under the throwback provision, sales by a company in other states in which the company pays no taxes (because it has no property or employees there) are counted as sales within the originating state. Membership is indicated in Table 14. Many of the non-members are located in the Northeast, where, as we shall see in the following chapter, the wasteful competition to offer tax incentives is most acute. If all states were members of these compacts, and if all states allocated income in the same way, then all companies would pay taxes on 100 percent of their taxable income, albeit at different rates, reflecting the different tax rates in different states. At present, 82 out-of-state sales by companies in non-compact states with neither employees nor property out-of-state represent a major tax exemption. Non-membership in a tax compact should properly be regarded as a tax incentive.

The allocation system is inequitable not only because it includes sales, but also because of the way that the treatment of each of the factors differs among states. New York, Florida, and Massachusetts double-weight sales, reducing the portion of taxable income on which state taxes are paid by the hypothetical company cited above from 52.8 percent to 42.5 percent. Minnesota allows companies the option of weighting sales by 70 percent, and payroll and property by 15 percent each. Wisconsin allows either double weighting of sales, or two-thirds to sales and one-third to either property or payrolls. In addition, New York does not count executive personnel payrolls in the state as part of the state's share of the payroll, thus favoring headquarters establishments over production facilities. The Tax Compact has failed to bring uniformity to state tax codes principally because states fear the loss of tax revenues or the loss of a tax incentive (Cahoon and Brown, 1973).

An even more complex allocation issue is how to treat multinational corporations and their affiliates (ACIR, 1975; Ebel, 1978; and Hellerstein, 1976). Businesses argue that U.S.-based affiliates should be treated as separate entities with transactions with other units of the firm treated on an "arms length" basis, with each affiliate computing its own profits. However, this is expensive administratively—it is difficult to compute prices of goods sold between affiliates—and it ignores the inherent economic advantages of multinationals, which are, after all, formed to take advantage of the fact that they can cooperate more cheaply than if they were separate entities. California, Oregon, and Alaska attempt to treat corporations as unitary wholes. This issue must be addressed in the near future.

Shift Between Business and Households   Due (1961) has argued that more harmful than high taxes themselves is the *belief* that taxes are influential (p. 171).

> The endless propaganda on the subject and strategy-inspired announcements of business firms when tax changes are being considered lead many legislators to exaggerate the influence of the taxes beyond any effect which they may have. The result is a potential danger of state cut-throat competition . . . In terror of "driving business out," legislatures become unwilling to adjust taxes to levels necessary to meet the desires of the community for services, and to bring their tax structures in line with popularly accepted ideas of equity in taxation.

These words sound depressingly prophetic. Cut-throat competition has become what Harrison and Kanter (1976) have called "The Great

State Robbery" (see following chapter), and an aversion to taxing businesses has led to residential taxes high enough to provoke the 2 to 1 passage of Proposition 13, and thriving fiscal limitations movements in most states (see Chapter 8).

Tax competition among states for business has shifted the tax burden from businesses to individuals. In 1948, personal income taxes provided 7.4 percent of states revenues, and corporate income taxes 8.7 percent. By 1977, while personal income taxes had swollen to 21.0 percent of states revenues, corporate income taxes had actually fallen to 7.6 percent.

Of course, all taxes are ultimately paid by households. The important question is what household activities and characteristics determine the amount of taxes paid. The corporate income tax is paid, at least in the "first round," by the owners of capital (stockholders) and the consumers of the product of the corporation. The personal income tax is paid by those working, and thus tends to discourage labor force participation. The personal income tax may be less progressive than the corporate income tax inasmuch as the ownership of capital tends to be concentrated among the relatively well-off. The net effect of the shift from the corporate income tax to the personal income tax has been to increase the regressivity of the tax system.

ADMINISTRATIVE COST

Administratively, the most convenient taxes are those that are simple add-ons to federal taxes, such as personal and business income taxes and the motor fuel tax, providing that the state employs the same tax base definition as the federal government. The property tax and sales tax involve much greater local efforts. Table 15 shows the ranking of major taxes with respect to their revenue predictability, stabilizing influence, and growth rate, averaged across all states. In terms of revenue growth, the local property tax out performs all state taxes during periods of inflation (Greytak and Jump, 1975). However, its salad days have been numbered by the taxpayer revolt. As might be expected, predictable taxes tend not to exert a strong stabilizing influence. States tend to select a tax package that balances these characteristics.

Companies operating in more than one state face special administrative problems due to the different taxing practices of the states. As Senator Abraham Ribicoff has argued: "The present system of state taxation is so unwieldly, so cumbersome, that many companies, particularly smaller ones, simply do not have the ability to meet the taxing requirements of all the jurisdictions in whch their goods are sold" (*Congressional Record,* S. 4850, March 15, 1973). This legal nightmare requires simplification.

Table 15
Stability, Growth, and Stabilizing Influence
of Selected State Tax Revenues

Tax	Stability of Revenues: Rank	Annual Growth Rate (per cent)	Stabilization Effect: Rank
Motor Fuel	1	5.9	3
Vehicle License	2	5.9	7
Sales	3	7.6	2
Alcoholic Beverage	4	6.0	6
Tobacco	5	8.4	5
Individual Income	6	11.8	4
Corporate Income	7	7.2	1

SOURCE: Adapted from William V. Williams et al., "The Stability, Growth and Stabilizing Influence of State Taxes," *National Tax Journal,* Vol. XXVI, No. 2 1973, p. 271.

WHAT SHOULD STATES DO?

The preceding discussion has revealed a number of problems with the present structure of business taxes. Taking steps to improve the system necessarily involves a leap of judgment, for we really do not understand the operation of the tax system. Improvement appears possible in a number of areas:

■ First, states should resist the tendency to cut business taxes to further economic development. In fact, a strong argument can be made to shift some of the state tax burden from individuals onto businesses.
■ Second, states should take steps to reduce interjurisdictional differences in business tax rates.
■ Third, states should review their allocation formulas for firms operating in more than one state.
■ Fourth, states should consider a Value Added Tax to replace complex business taxes.
■ Fifth, states should consider encouraging local jurisdictions to increase the tax rate on land relative to property improvements.

These issues are discussed in turn below.

Overall Tax Levels We have argued that overall business tax levels have little impact on regional economic growth, although intrastate differences may lead to the migration of some companies out of high taxing central cities to suburban or exurban areas. States should review their state/local tax structure to ensure that it does not discriminate heavily against certain types of industry, and adjust it so that it is not significantly out-of-line with neighboring states. George Roniger (1978) of Citibank has argued, "because of technical progress, business, economic activity and jobs are no longer captive of any particular area. The ability of any government to extract an economic rent becomes daily less." States should lower taxes that are competitively out-of-line and let the market determine which industries will thrive, rather than tampering with the tax system to save a particular industry. Perhaps the most important guide should be the administrative savings of bringing taxes in line or simplifying the tax structure.

However, they should resist pressure to reduce business taxes to stimulate development, and should consider increasing the burden on industry relative to households. In large part, this could be done by closing many of the special tax loopholes that not only reduce the average tax burden on business but also create considerable inequity among businesses by favoring a relatively few large businesses which are not the main source of local job creation. After all, businesses enjoy only about half of the advantage of low local taxes—the rest goes to the federal government in the form of increased federal taxes.

Interstate Tax Allocation There seems little chance that states acting individually, or through the Tax Compact, will make much progress in simplifying the taxation of multi-state businesses. A fear of revenue loss prevents the necessary steps from being taken. Federal legislation is needed to resolve the complex jurisdictional questions, particularly in the sales and use tax area, that have led to the present inequitable and inefficient system (Cahoon and Brown, 1973).

Interjurisdictional Tax Differences More important than aggregate state tax levels are the wide tax variations—particularly in business property tax rates—among jurisdictions. Firms have moved away from high taxing central city locations toward suburban and even exurban areas. Much of this tax-induced movement does not reflect an efficiency gain but a response to the internal biases of the tax structure, and has tended to exacerbate the problems of fiscally troubled jurisdictions and multiply the benefits of growing areas.

86 In the previous chapter we outlined a number of steps that state

governments could take to reduce fiscal inequities, steps that would help reduce the kind of disparities that have contributed to local economic problems.

The redistribution of fiscal burdens among jurisdictions should aim at complete equalization of tax burdens and services. It should be concerned with reducing the disparity of resources so that local areas can choose the quality and quantity of public services they wish. One major advantage of the state/local fiscal structure is that it allows local differentiation on the basis of local preferences. Redistribution can help to ensure that poor areas are not as constrained in their choices as they would be without aid.

Value Added Tax[8]

One alternative to the complex array of business taxes that many states and localities employ is a tax on value-added, patterned on the Michigan single business tax. The corporate income tax has several disadvantages. It is highly volatile. During recessions many firms earn no taxable income—and investment decisions by large firms may also sharply reduce taxable income. Revenues are, therefore, very difficult to predict. It is also complex to administer, and may discourage investment.

The value added tax, as applied in Michigan, is basically a tax on gross sales minus purchases of inputs from other companies. The computation of the tax base is:

> *Add*   Federal taxable income
> + total compensation paid
> + interest paid
> + dividends paid
> + depreciation[9]
> + lease rent payments
>
> *Subtract*   Interest received
> − dividends received
> − capital purchases[9]

There are several modifications that are used in the Michigan structure introduced in 1976. Some of the more important are:

■ A standard deduction of $34,000 prevents a proliferation of small tax returns.
■ Gross receipts limitation. The VAT base cannot exceed 50 percent of gross receipts.
■ Total compensation is limited to 65 percent of the tax base (35 percent for food retailers and private security guards). **87**

■ Rental real estate. Taxpayers whose interest and depreciation exceed 70 percent of base are allowed to limit their base to 35 percent of gross receipts.

■ For financial institutions, interest received is *added* to the base and interest paid is *deducted.*

Who would benefit and who would lose from the introduction of a Michigan-type single business tax would depend on the taxes replaced and the specific provisions of the new tax. Some impression of the intersectoral shifts that may occur can be gained from some calculations performed by Cropper for a similar (but not identical) tax in New York City (Table 16, col. 2). The studies agree in the following general conclusions: Sectors experiencing a large *increase* in tax liabilities include construction, some manufacturing, and wholesale; those experiencing the most dramatic declines would be finance and some manufacturing. Among manufacturing industries, both studies agree that apparel, furniture, and leather would experience increased liabilities, while chemicals, instruments, and non-electrical machinery would face reduced liabilities. We cannot predict the employment change that would result from these hypothesized changes in tax liability. However, we can make the following qualitative observations:

■ In the manufacturing sector, taxes are reduced on industries that tend to be growing more rapidly nationally, while taxes are raised on declining industries. For growth industries, this may allow an area to capture a greater share of firm births and relocations, and encourage existing companies to grow more rapidly.

■ The high rate paid by services and retail will raise local prices, although some of the service burden will be exported. Some compensating reduction in the retail sales tax may be necessary. The in creased burden on medical and legal services may have a negative effect on city development.

Administratively, the Michigan experience favors the VAT. An ACIR (1977) study cites the Michigan Department of Treasury as concluding that, after a transition period, the administrative costs of the VAT will be less than those of the old tax system, and litigation costs will decline. Although its introduction was opposed by business, there has been no move to repeal it.

The corporate income tax is based on a firm's ability to pay. The VAT tax is more closely related to the value of public services received. The VAT base is a measure of the level of business activity—such as payroll—which, it is agreed, is proportional to the value of
88 local public services received—such as roads, police, and fire

Table 16
Two Estimates of the Percentage Change in Tax Liability by Sector
as a Result of Replacing the Corporate Income Tax
with a Value Added Tax

Sector	Change in Liability as Percent of Initial Liability	
	Cropper	Aaron
Agriculture	NA	+1524
Transport	+29*	+135
Oil and Gas	NA	+222
Services	-25	+330
Construction	+90	+346
Lumber	NA	+97
Amusements	NA	+80
Trade	NA	+75
Wholesale	+100	NA
Retail	-2	NA
Auto Repair	NA	+395
Food	+22	-15
Leather	+200	+26
Furniture	+150	+9
Textiles	0	+8
Metal Products	+38	+3
Metal Mining	NA	+8
Coal	NA	-5
Coal	NA	-5
Metals	NA	-11
Rubber	+50	-3
Misc. Manufacturing	-22	-19
Home Appliances	+8	-18
Printing	+45	-13
Machinery	-38	-36
Paper	+17	-41
Instruments	-10	-44
Finance	-35	-47
Ordnance	NA	-51
Tobacco	NA	-58
Radio and TV	NA	-57
Chemical	-35	-60
Automobiles	NA	-65
Communications	NA*	-59
Utilities	NA*	-72

SOURCE: Henry Aaron, "Differential Price Effects of a Value Added Tax," *National Tax Journal,* Vol. 21, No. 2, 1968, pp. 162-175; Maureen Cropper, "The Value Added Tax as Alternative to the General Corporation and Unincorporated Business Tax," New York City Finance Administration, August 1970.

NA means not available.

*Transport includes communications and utilities

protection.

The *advantages* of the VAT are:

■ It reduces taxes on relatively footloose growth industries in manufacturing, and on the rapidly growing financial sector, and increases it on captive firms.
■ It is easier to forecast revenues and is a stable source of revenues.
■ It reduces the tax disincentive on capital investment by distributing the burden across all factors of production.
■ It is administratively more simple than the combination taxes it replaces.

The *disadvantages* are:

■ Transition could be disruptive.
■ The retail, wholesale and special services sectors would experience a sharp increase in taxes. Special services (medical, legal, etc.) are a major source of urban employment growth.

Table 17 summarizes the difference between the Michigan Value Added Tax and more traditional business taxes.

Site Value Taxation

An alternative to property taxation that is receiving growing attention is land value taxation—a tax on the value of land exclusive of any building improvement.[10] The present property tax is a combination of two taxes, one on land—the value of location—and the second is a tax on the value of improvements. The tax on improvements discourages new property investment, while the tax on vacant land is so small that speculators leave many vacant lots unimproved.[11]

Land value taxation is politically feasible. Municipalities in Australia and New Zealand use land value taxation. In Pennsylvania, several cities have used their authority for land value taxation for municipal levies, but are limited to taxing land values at twice the rate levied on buildings. School and county levies are excluded. Moreover, state legislative proposals have been introduced to extend the use of land value taxes.

A case study of the impact of the land value taxation in Sydney, Australia endorses its effectiveness (Archer, 1972). The study concluded that the most important aspect of the tax was that it put pressure "on owners to sell their property for redevelopment if they cannot or will not develop it themselves." This is accomplished by the cash outflow required by the site value system (p. 38). This also:

90 ■ Promotes a more active and informed market in redevelopment

Table 17
Comparison of the Michigan Value Added Tax
to the Typical State Business Tax Structure

Issues	Typical State Structure	Michigan Value Added Tax
Composition	Complex—relies on many tax bases such as corporate, partnership, and sole proprietorship income, capital value, business inventory.	Simpler—replaces income, capital value, and franchise bases with the value added.[1]
Philosophy	Emphasis on net profits of business firm, therefore related to *ability* to pay.	Emphasis on business activity (use of capital and labor), therefore more closely related to *benefits received.*
Uniformity of Treatment of Business Firms	Scores poorly because the tax liability of the firm often depends on the form of business organization, i.e., whether or not the firm is incorporated.	Scores well on uniformity— businesses are taxed on basis of economic size rather than form of business organization.
Uniformity of Treatment of Capital and Labor	Taxes fall more heavily on capital than on labor—net profits, inventories, and net worth taxes in particular. Income of corporation is taxed not only when earned but also when distributed to shareholders.	No bias against capital because the impact of the tax is on capital and labor in proportion to their contribution to the value added to the product.
Incentive for Increased Capital Investment	Not available unless provided by special treatment such as accelerated depreciation or investment credit.	No inherent discrimination against capital. One benefit-may reduce pressure to grant special concessions.
Stability of Revenue	Heavy reliance on income tax base results in sensitivity of collections to changes in the economy. To taxpayers this appears as an advantage, because lower profits result in lower tax liability.	Inclusion in the tax base of compensation to labor results in more stability in tax liability. To taxpayers this appears as a disadvantage, because taxes must be paid even if no profits are earned.

[1]Local real estate and personal property taxes on machinery and equpment are still paid by Michigan businesses.

SOURCE: Compiled by ACIR staff, and reproduced in the Advisory Commission for Intergovernmental Relations, *The Michigan Single Business Tax,* Washington, D.C., March 1978.

properties.

■ Facilitates the consolidation of smaller sites.

■ Allows developers to expand their role in the redevelopment building market at the expense of single project redevelopment by property owners.

Transition to a site value tax system involves considerable disruption. It should, therefore, be carried out slowly. In fact, the site value tax need not be regarded as an alternative to the property tax, but as merely a modification. The rate on land could be raised relative to that on buildings; the tax on improvements need not be reduced to zero. In many areas, this may only bring into line a property tax which frequently taxes land at a lower rate than improvements. However, Hawaii, which introduced a modified site value tax in 1963, intending to slowly raise the rate on land relative to buildings, found the process too cumbersome and repealed the differential tax in July 1978. Although the Tax Foundation of Hawaii argued the differential was ineffective, another recent study estimated that had a significant differential been tried, it would have reduced sprawl (Pollock and Shoup, 1977). The tax was recommended for New York (Finkelstein, 1975), but rejected for the District of Columbia (Peterson, 1978). Opponents argue that zoning, removal of red tape, and land assembly grants are more effective incentives than a differential rate on land and improvements. Many jurisdictions already assess land and improvements separately. The rate on land could be steadily increased while that on improvements is reduced. A temporary circuit breaker could be used to ensure that no one experienced radical annual changes in tax payments.

The problem with implementing a land value tax is that there are relatively few unimproved land sites that change hands in any year from which estimates of surrounding land values could be assessed. However, it is possible, by regression analysis of full property values (land plus buildings), to estimate the contribution of site value to total value. This change, therefore, requires relatively sophisticated assessment techniques, a practice that few jurisdictions have adopted. However, Oldman and Teachout (1977) conclude that even the most sophisticated assessment technique "could not withstand court appeal by an aggrieved taxpayer, because none adequately establishes (according to the criteria employed by courts) the market value of the land underlying individual properties" (Ebel, 1978, p. 7). But, they argue, legal and administrative remedies are potentially available to make the tax operational.

In addition, there is some dispute concerning the equity of the change. Landowners of property with a high ratio of improvements to land value—owners of office buildings, hotels, theaters, and some manufacturing—would receive a tax reduction, while single family homes and the owners of vacant land would experience a tax increase.

The site value tax, or an increase in the tax on land, may not be efficient in all places. Rapidly growing areas are most likely to benefit, since they experience the greatest problem with land speculation. For example, areas that already effectively assess land will benefit less than those that under-assess land. Also, those jurisdictions that have introduced tax abatement or exemption on any increases in property values have removed much of the disincentive impact of the property tax. Peterson (1978) estimates this is equivalent to a 25 percent reduction in the cost of capital, but concludes that this has not been a major incentive and that cash grants on improvements have been more effective. Also, in many jurisdictions, vacant land is effectively taxed at rates well below the rate on improvements due to poor assessment techniques. Simply enforcing a uniform rate, as is mandated in almost all jurisdictions, would improve the equity and efficiency of the tax. While there are potential problems with a site value tax, or an increase in the tax on land relative to improvements, it is an option that merits further consideration.

FOOTNOTES TO CHAPTER 5

1. These are Nevada, Ohio, South Dakota, Texas and Washington. In addition, some cities have local corporate income taxes. The large cities are:

Ohio		Michigan	
Akron	1.5 percent	Detroit	2.0 percent
Cincinnati	2.0 percent	Flint	1.0 percent
Cleveland	1.0 percent	Grand Rapids	1.0 percent
Columbus	1.5 percent	Lansing	1.0 percent
Dayton	1.75 percent		
Toledo	1.5 percent	Kentucky	
Youngstown	1.5 percent	Louisville	2.2 percent
Missouri		New York	
Kansas City	1.0 percent	New York City	9.5 percent
St. Louis	1.0 percent		
		Oregon	
		Multnomah County	0.6 percent

2. This is different from a retail sales tax, which taxes retail sales regardless of where the goods are produced.

3. Iowa has no business income tax but taxes the gross value of sales. Michigan has a tax on value added (see this chapter, below).

4. An inverse example is provided by the time when tea duties were slashed in the late nineteenth century by the British government: revenues rose because smuggling became unprofitable.

5. "Relatively concentrated" means that employment in these industries employs a higher share of the city's labor force than they do of the nation's labor.

6. Iowa is one exception—it uses a single factor—gross sales.

7. The Multistate Tax Compact and the Uniform Division of Income for Tax Assessment.

8. The Value Added Tax in Michigan replaced not only the corporate income tax, but also a corporate franchise tax, an inventory tax, a business intangible tax, a financial corporations tax, an insurance company and a savings and loan company privilege tax.

9. There are three forms of VAT that differ in the way they treat depreciation:
■ *Consumption VAT:* deducts purchases of capital equipment but does tax depreciation.
■ *Net Income VAT:* taxes capital equipment when purchased but does not tax depreciation (i.e., assumes 100 percent depreciation in the first year).
■ *Gross Product VAT:* Taxes both capital purchases and depreciation.

10. See Becker (1969); Carlson (1977); Cuddington (1978); and testimony before the House Committee on Banking, Currency and Housing by Lowell Harris, George Peterson, Philip Finkelstein, and Arthur Becker, September 28, 1976, reprinted by the Committee in *Rebirth of the American City,* U.S. House of Representatives, Washington, D.C., 1976.

11. In the 1950s, the lot comprised about 10 percent of the cost of a home; today, it is 25 percent (Carlson, 1977).

6

WHAT SHOULD STATES DO ABOUT TAX INCENTIVES?

A direct result of the belief that business taxes really matter has been the proliferation of special tax incentives designed by states and localities to attract new businesses and to encourage expansion and new investment among existing firms. There are no reliable estimates as to how much in tax receipts are currently foregone under these programs. Smokestack chasing is *de rigeur* for states that adopt an aggressive development program. However, the clear conclusion of this chapter is that, for the most part, *firms are rewarded for doing what they would have done even in the absence of the incentive.* The fixation of states and localities on attracting manufacturing firms by whatever fiscal means possible has arisen from the belief that a new firm will yield a fiscal surplus—that is, its contribution to local tax revenues outweighs the costs of providing public services to the firm and its employees (Groves and Riew, 1963; and Kee, 1968). More recent studies, however, have shown that a new firm is not an unmixed blessing. Even in a community with relative high unemployment, 100 new jobs does not reduce local unemployment by 100. At least 50 of those slots are likely to be filled by new inmigrants who will require schooling, streets, sewers, and water. Other jobs might be filled by those not previously in the labor force. Secondary employment—retail and services—will also make demands for public services and do not necessarily yield a fiscal surplus. In fact, Gerweck and Epp (1976) show that secondary employment impacts may halve the net fiscal surplus resulting from a new factory. *When the state abates or exempts local taxes to induce a firm to move in, the net benefits may well become negative.*

The adoption of tax incentives tailored to the wishes of the few Fortune 500 companies that move is based on the mistaken belief that there is a fixed stock of manufacturing jobs in the nation and that the only way a state can improve its relative position is to steal from other states. The behavior is analagous to that of the homeowner who tries to maintain a green lawn by stealing his neighbors turf—at great effort —every time his own land turns brown. It is much easier and more productive to water regularly and apply fertilizer. We should reiterate the conclusions from earlier chapters. There are very few footloose firms. If growth is to be accelerated, then it must come from increasing the local company birth rate or from expansion in existing local companies, especially small firms. *Development efforts must focus upon* **95**

Table 18

Financial Assistance, Tax Incentives, and Special Services Offered by State and Local Governments

FINANCIAL ASSISTANCE

State	State Sponsored Industrial Development Authority	Privately Sponsored Development Credit Corporation	State Authority or Agency Revenue Bond Financing	State Authority or Agency General Obligation Bond Financing	City and/or County Revenue Bond Financing	City and/or County General Obligation Bond Financing	State Loans for Building Construction	State Loans for Equipment/Machinery	City and/or County Loans for Building Construction	City and/or County Loans for Equipment/Machinery	State Loan Guarantees for Building Construction	State Loan Guarantees for Equipment/Machinery	City and/or County Loan Guarantees for Building Construction	City and/or County Loan Guarantee for Equipment/Machinery	State Financing Aid for Existing Plant Expansions	State Matching Funds for City and/or County Industrial Financing Programs	State Incentive for Establishing Industrial Plants in Areas of High Unemployment	City and/or County Incentive for Establishing Industrial Plants in Areas of High Unemployment
Alabama	•	•			•										•			
Alaska	•	•		•	•	•	•	•							•			
Arizona					•													
Arkansas	•	•			•	•					•							
California		•															•	
Colorado					•													
Connecticut	•	•	•	•	•	•	•	•	•	•	•	•	•	•	•	•	•	
Delaware	•		•	•	•	•					•	•						
Florida		•			•													
Georgia		•	•		•													
Hawaii	•		•		•	•	•								•		•	
Idaho																		
Illinois	•	•			•		•	•							•			
Indiana	•	•			•						•	•			•		•	
Iowa		•			•													
Kansas		•			•	•												
Kentucky	•	•			•	•	•								•			
Louisiana	•				•													
Maine	•	•			•						•	•			•			
Maryland	•	•			•						•	•			•	•	•	
Massachusetts		•			•				•	•	•				•		•	•
Michigan	•	•			•		•				•	•			•	•		
Minnesota	•	•			•		•	•	•	•					•			
Mississippi	•	•			•	•									•			•
Missouri		•			•	•		•							•			•
Montana		•			•					•					•			
Nebraska		•			•										•			
Nevada					•	•											•	•
New Hampshire	•	•	•		•		•				•	•			•			
New Jersey		•	•		•	•	•				•	•			•	•	•	•
New Mexico	•				•	•												
New York	•	•	•		•		•								•			
North Carolina					•													
North Dakota	•	•	•		•		•								•		•	
Ohio	•	•			•		•				•	•			•			
Oklahoma	•	•			•	•	•	•	•						•			
Oregon	•	•			•										•	•	•	
Pennsylvania	•	•	•		•			•							•			•
Rhode Island	•	•	•		•						•	•			•			
South Carolina	•	•	•		•													
South Dakota					•													
Tennessee	•		•		•	•					•	•			•			
Texas	•				•	•		•							•			
Utah	•	•			•													
Vermont	•	•			•		•	•			•	•			•	•	•	•
Virginia	•	•			•													
Washington	•	•			•	•				•								
West Virginia	•	•			•		•		•	•					•	•	•	•
Wisconsin					•	•												
Wyoming		•			•													
STATE TOTALS	32	34	29	7	45	21	19	13	8	7	14	13	1	1	29	9	17	10

Table 18 *(continued)*

TAX INCENTIVES   SPECIAL SERVICES

1. Corporate Income Tax Exemption
2. Personal Income Tax Exemption
3. Excise Tax Exemption
4. Tax Exemption or Moratorium on Land, Capital Improvements
5. Tax Exemption or Moratorium on Equipment, Machinery
6. Inventory Tax Exemption on Goods in Transit (Freeport)
7. Tax Exemptions on Manufacturers' Inventories
8. Sales/Use Tax Exemption on New Equipment
9. Tax Exemption on Raw Materials Used in Manufacture
10. Tax Credits for Use of Specified State Products
11. Tax Stabilization Agreements for Specified Industries
12. Tax Exemption to Encourage Research and Development
13. Accelerated Depreciation of Industrial Equipment
14. State Financed Speculative Building
15. City and/or County Financed Speculative Building
16. Cities and/or Counties Provide Free Land for Industry
17. State-Owned Industrial Park Sites
18. City and/or County-Owned Industrial Park Sites
19. State Funds for City and or County Development Related Public Works Projects
20. State Funds for City and or County Master Plans
21. State Funds for City and or County Recreational Projects

1	2	3	4	5	6	7	8	9	10	11	12	13	14	15	16	17	18	19	20	21	STATE TOTALS	State
●	●	●	●		●	●	●	●						●	●	●	●	●	●	●	21	Alabama
						●	●	●		●							●	●	●	●	14	Alaska
●	●			●	●		●					●					●	●	●	●	11	Arizona
				●	●	●	●							●			●		●	●	13	Arkansas
				●	●		●					●					●	●	●	●	9	California
				●	●		●					●		●	●		●	●	●	●	10	Colorado
●			●	●	●		●				●						●	●	●	●	26	Connecticut
		●		●	●		●	●				●					●	●	●	●	19	Delaware
●	●				●		●	●	●								●				9	Florida
			●	●	●	●	●	●				●		●			●	●	●	●	14	Georgia
●	●			●	●	●	●	●				●				●	●	●	●	●	19	Hawaii
					●	●	●	●				●					●	●		●	8	Idaho
		●			●		●	●				●					●	●	●	●	14	Illinois
			●		●		●	●				●			●		●	●	●	●	17	Indiana
●					●		●	●				●					●				7	Iowa
●				●	●		●	●				●		●	●		●				14	Kansas
●				●	●	●	●	●				●					●	●	●	●	16	Kentucky
●				●	●	●	●	●	●			●			●		●			●	14	Louisiana
					●	●	●			●	●	●	●	●			●				16	Maine
			●		●		●	●			●	●	●				●	●		●	20	Maryland
●				●	●		●				●	●		●			●	●	●	●	21	Massachusetts
	●			●	●		●							●	●		●	●	●	●	18	Michigan
●	●	●	●		●	●	●	●		●	●						●	●	●	●	25	Minnesota
	●			●	●	●	●	●				●		●	●	●	●				18	Mississippi
●				●	●		●	●				●					●				13	Missouri
●					●		●										●		●	●	12	Montana
					●		●							●			●		●	●	10	Nebraska
●	●																●				9	Nevada
	●			●	●		●	●				●		●			●	●	●	●	19	New Hampshire
				●	●		●	●			●	●		●	●		●	●	●	●	24	New Jersey
					●		●	●							●		●				8	New Mexico
●	●	●	●		●		●				●			●			●	●	●	●	27	New York
					●	●	●					●		●	●		●	●	●	●	10	North Carolina
●	●			●	●		●				●			●	●		●	●		●	23	North Dakota
●	●			●	●		●										●		●	●	21	Ohio
	●			●	●	●	●	●			●			●	●		●	●	●	●	23	Oklahoma
●	●	●		●	●		●					●					●	●	●	●	19	Oregon
				●	●		●					●		●			●	●	●	●	20	Pennsylvania
				●	●		●	●		●	●						●	●	●	●	18	Rhode Island
				●	●	●	●	●				●			●		●		●	●	15	South Carolina
●	●	●	●		●									●	●		●	●		●	12	South Dakota
	●			●	●	●	●		●			●		●		●	●	●	●	●	22	Tennessee
●	●			●	●	●		●									●	●	●	●	15	Texas
					●	●		●									●				7	Utah
					●		●	●		●		●	●				●	●	●	●	22	Vermont
	●			●	●		●		●			●		●			●	●	●	●	14	Virginia
●	●			●	●		●	●									●	●		●	16	Washington
●	●	●			●		●					●			●		●	●	●	●	19	West Virginia
●				●	●	●	●	●				●					●	●	●	●	13	Wisconsin
●	●	●		●	●	●	●										●	●		●	10	Wyoming
21	19	10	23	38	41	37	33	44	3	4	9	25	5	29	14	8	47	34	31	38		STATE TOTALS

SOURCE: Adapted from "The Fifty Legislative Climates," *Industrial Development,* January/February 1978.

Note that the form in which states offer financial services, tax incentives, and special services differ widely. For a full description see the original source.

the overall economic climate, not upon expensive incentives to a few firms.[1]

Business incentive programs are designed not only to attract footloose industries but also to encourage existing firms to expand their level of operations to generate jobs locally. However, as we argued in the preceding chapter, high local business income and property taxes have not had much influence on investment decisions, and, therefore, temporary reductions as a reward for purchasing additional equipment are unlikely to have much impact. In fact, we will argue that reducing the tax on the income from capital to create jobs is perverse, since the policy does nothing to reduce the cost of labor. If a state insists on using tax incentives to generate employment, and we cannot hold out much hope for their effectiveness, it should try to counter the impacts of payroll taxes by introducing wage subsidies.

A systematic examination of business incentives is a large undertaking because of their bewildering variety. For example, we argued in the preceding chapter that the double weighting of out-of-state sales and non-membership in tax compacts should be considered as tax incentives. Table 18 lists some of the financial services, tax incentives, and special programs provided by states for firms. The incentives include exemptions from personal and corporate income tax for those firms moving in, guarantees that property taxes will not increase for 5 or 10 years, exemption of new manufacturing equipment from the sales tax, and accelerated depreciation. Special services encompass free land for industry, state funds for research and development, and state help in bidding on federal procurement contracts. Financial assistance runs from tax exempt revenue bond financing to state matching funds for local development efforts. The discussion in this chapter focuses mainly upon tax incentives, but some of these other development measures are also briefly discussed.

A review of aggressive promotion campaigns by states and cities reveals just how internecine the competition has become.[2] New York State advertises that "We're not giving business the business any more. We're giving it a break", Chicago claims to be "Fund City", and San Diego "is zoned for success," according to its $500,000 a year campaign. The Texas Industrial Commission advises, "When the old corporate tax bite eats away profits, CUT OUT FOR TEXAS." In 1977, nearly $7 million was spent in magazines alone, and the number of business promotion ads jumped by 40 percent in the first three months of 1978.

The rivalry for footloose industries has often been cast as the old and established Snowbelt trying to protect its economic base from the aggressive inroads of the tax cutting Sunbelt. The truth is very different. The fiercest rivalry is between adjacent states—a cut-throat regional struggle that mortgages future tax receipts and places established factories at a disadvantage relative to the brash newcomers. Ohio and Pennsylvania rival for Volkswagen, while steel companies languish. Firms leave New York State for adjacent Connecticut, New Jersey, and Pennsylvania. Most of the states offering twenty or more special programs (cf. Table 18) are in the Northeast.[3] In fact, public pressure for such measures is most intense in states where the economic development rate has been slower than the national average. A recent survey by the Advisory Commission on Intergovernmental Relations (1977) suggests that public support for tax incentives for business is closely related to local economic fortunes and prospects.

Question: Some states have passed laws which give special tax breaks or other incentives to industries that will locate facilities or expand present operations in that state. Do you favor or oppose such a policy?

| | Percent of Total U.S. | Percent of Respondents by Region | | | |
		Northeast	North Central	South	West
Favor	50	57	48	52	42
Oppose	36	30	38	30	49
No Opinion	14	13	13	18	9

SOURCE: ACIR, *Changing Public Attitudes on Government and Taxes,* Washington, D.C., 1977.

If this wasteful competition is to cease, state officials must educate their constituents about the futility of these programs.

EFFICIENCY

Do tax incentives work? Do they attract new firms and encourage new investment? There is no evidence that these concessions have had any significant effect on local growth.[4] Tax concessions are ineffective precisely because state and local taxes are, themselves, relatively unimportant as location determinants.

The tax battle is not only waged between states, but between counties and municipalities within a state. County officials offered a new bicarbonate plant a 12 year property tax break for moving to Seneca County, Ohio, yet the corporation's controller was quoted as saying, "The tax abatement was a nice kicker on the end, but we chose Ohio mainly because of its strategic location for distribution and market growth."[5]

Weinstein (1977, p. 75) concludes that:

Taken as a whole, these incentives probably represent a serious misallocation of resources. In the main the government is subsidizing firms **99** for performing activities they would have undertaken in any case. Furthermore, when one considers that any incentive designed to reduce a company's state or local tax bill will increase that firm's federal tax liability—the superfluity of tax incentives becomes even more apparent. The result is a form of reverse revenue sharing in the amount of 48 cents on the dollar.

Even if local investment expanded by 2 percent as a result of a local investment tax credit, this still means that 98 percent of credits are flowing to firms that would have invested anyway.

Not only are tax incentives ineffective, they are also costly. Harrison and Kanter (1976) estimate that the ten tax incentives offered by Massachusetts cost at least $100 million a year, revenues that could be used to reduce residential taxes or improve local services. In just over a year, New York City has exempted $461 million in properties from $44 million in taxes. St. Louis has exempted nearly $1 billion worth of real estate—half the city's property tax base. By the early 1980s, Michigan's incentives may cost $50 million in state revenues and $30 million in local revenues.

Of course, to determine whether a measure is worthwhile, it is important to compare its benefits with its costs. A local development incentive does not have to be very effective to be worthwhile if its costs are negligible. The few studies that have compared the costs and benefits of fiscal incentives do not provide a very optimistic picture, although they do show that, under some conditions, fiscal incentives may be cost effective. Morgan and Hackbart (1974) concluded that if locally accruing benefits are not less than 50 percent of value added in a local plant and not less than 5 percent of the investment is a result of an incentive, then that incentive may be cost effective from the viewpoint of the state, although, as we argued in Chapter 2, there is no guarantee that the nation as a whole is not worse off.

What of the few firms that may respond to some kind of fiscal incentive?[6] Are they the type of firm that can assist meeting local development goals? In an important article, Harrison and Kanter (1976) argue that the type of firm most likely to respond are firms in highly competitive industries, for whom small differences in costs make the difference between success and failure. Yet, they argue:

> . . . these are the industries that in general pay lower wages, offer worse working conditions, provide less stable employment, and make it more difficult for labor to organize. Thus, incentives that lower costs of doing business appear to be policy instruments—if they work at all—that are most likely to "goose" the sector of the economy with the least desirable jobs, while providing windfall profits to the segments of the business community that needs them the least (p. 59).

In short, tax incentives are ineffective, and what little impact they might have is not necessarily desirable.

EQUITY Not only are tax incentives inefficient, they are also inequitable. First, the incentive will tend to go to large and financially healthy firms, since these firms will be earning a taxable income.[7] Nearly 50 percent of all firms had no federal tax liability in 1971, and 95 percent of all firms had federal tax liabilities of less than $25,000 (Table 19). Unless the incentives take the form of credits, most firms will not be influenced.

Second, why should a new company pay less in taxes than a comparable firm that is well established in the state? State policy makers should be aware that this program may harm their well established firms, by placing them at a competitive disadvantage with newer competitors locating in other tax cutting states.

A third equity problem is that state and local officials often weave

Table 19
Cumulative Distributions of Income Tax Liabilities
for Corporations Filing Income Tax Returns
in 1971, by Sector

Sector	Income Tax Liability		
	0	Below $10,000	Below $25,000
All Industries	49.0	90.5	94.8
Agriculture	53.3	94.2	97.8
Mining	61.2	86.6	91.8
Contract Construction	50.9	91.0	95.3
Manufacturing	48.4	82.4	87.8
Transportation and Communication and Utilities	53.1	90.6	94.5
Wholesale and Retail	43.1	88.7	94.2
Fire	47.3	92.1	95.9
Services	56.5	95.7	98.1

SOURCE: Robert Tannenwald, "Federal Tax Approaches to Regional Development," in Committee on Appropriations, *Patterns of Regional Change,* U.S. Senate, Washington, D.C., October 1977, p. 697.

together a special "development package" for a particular firm that is considering moving in, threatening to move out, or considering a major expansion. Naturally, officials can only do so if the firm is large. Programs can rarely reach down to small firms, even though past experience suggests that such firms are the main source of employment expansion.

A final equity issue is that almost all incentives are offered to the owners of capital; few are offered to labor. We have argued that payroll taxes and minimum wage laws have priced low-skilled labor out of jobs. It is possible to imagine that the long run impact of tax incentives might be to encourage the substitution of capital for labor and therefore to *reduce* the number of jobs, while enhancing the aggregate returns to the ownership of capital. If this impact is explicitly understood, enthusiasm for present tax incentives may diminish.

ADMINISTRATIVE COST

The effectiveness of tax incentives might be greater if they were targeted toward smaller firms, which are the main engines of local growth (Schmenner, 1978). However, while it is administratively simple to identify and approach the relatively few large companies that are considering relocation, the market of small firms is impossibly large. There is a much higher failure rate among small firms, and thus the risk of providing a financial assistance/tax incentive package to these firms is high, and the overall administrative cost is likely to be much higher.

OTHER BUSINESS INCENTIVE PROGRAMS

As Table 19 graphically shows, the menu offered to the lucky few businesses to arouse the interest of development officials is not limited to tinkering with the tax structure. The enterprising firm can enjoy low leases on publicly-built facilities, low interest rate loans, cash grants, and publicly-trained employees. Are these other measures more effective than tax incentives?

Our overall answer is that most of these programs are not of major importance to influencing company decisions. We can only touch on these programs briefly in this paper.[9]

Tax Exempt Bonds

A major problem with state and local efforts to attract or retain industry is that they rely upon tax expenditures—tax exemption of bond interest payments, for example—and that these are very inefficient ways of channeling subsidies to industry. The federal tax structure has exempted the interest from state and local bonds, as well as bonds sold by local public development corporations, from federal income tax.

State and local authorities have, for the most part, extended this exemption to local income taxes. There are several problems with this form of capital market subsidy.

First, only a part of the tax receipts foregone by the federal and state treasuries actually go to reduce borrowing costs. The remainder is a subsidy to high income bond holders. Estimates place the personal subsidy at between 25 percent and 30 percent of foregone revenues. Morris (1976) estimates that the tax exemption of bond interest cost the federal treasury $4.8 billion in 1976, of which only $3.5 billion effectively reduced state and local borrowing costs. Intramarginal bondholders—those with very high marginal income tax rates who would have been satisfied with a lower tax free yield—enjoyed a subsidy of $1.3 billion. Total state and local interest payments in that year were approximately $10.5 billion.

Second, the market for tax free bonds has been narrowing as investors turn to alternative shelters. At the same time, public issues have had to compete with pollution control bonds. Commercial banks purchased 90 percent of net purchases in 1968, but only 10 percent in 1975. The lowering of the maximum federal income tax rate on personal income in 1976 may have reduced the number of household buyers. Pollution control bonds, granted tax exempt status in 1969, grew from only $100 million in 1971 to $2.2 billion in 1975, a year when state and local governments issued $31.6 billion in long term debt.

Third, the interest on state and local bonds is much more volatile than on taxable issues. This volatility results from the selling of municipal bonds by banks during periods when alternatives become much more attractive. The price falls and yields rise to induce other investors to absorb these sales. For example, the average yield on Aa municipals rose from 62 percent of the yield on Aa corporate bonds in January 1968 to 73 percent in June of 1970. A similar shift occurred between 1973 and 1975. A period when inflationary expectations rise leads to more rapid increases in public borrowing costs than in private borrowing costs. Soaring interest rates deter necessary public investments.

Local Credit Agencies

Slow growth, it is popularly believed, may arise because of a shortage of loanable funds, or because of high interest rates. High interest rates apply nationwide, and although some regional variation is apparent (Straszheim, 1969), it is not significantly related to growth differences. The belief in a "credit-gap" has spawned a number of state and local practices that provide subsidized loans. Loan subsidies may be available through industrial development bonds, statewide industrial credit corporations, or state industrial finance corporations.

Industrial Development Bonds. Mississippi, in 1936, was the first state to authorize local industrial bonds. Local authorities are authorized to issue bonds to construct industrial facilities for lease to private firms. Interest on these bonds is exempt from federal and local income tax.[10] Aided firms pay rentals sufficient to cover the principal and interest on the bonds and facility maintenance. Facilities are generally exempt from state and local property taxation. Bonds may be secured by the taxing power of the issuing government (general obligation bonds) or by the property acquired with the bond revenue (revenue bonds).

Statewide Development Credit Corporations. Maine authorized the first state development credit corporation in 1969, and now 30 states have such corporations. These corporations are state chartered but privately financed, using revenues from stock sales, private borrowing, or from retained earnings. Their loans usually go to small, established manufacturing firms. Although most loans go for plant and equipment purchases, a sizable number do go for working capital. Almost all of these corporations have made profits. In all states except Alaska, local authorities have been permitted to set up development credit corporations.

There are now several thousand local development corporations concentrated in nonindustrialized areas and in industrialized areas with persistent, high unemployment rates. Some operate under the auspices of local chambers of commerce, others under local jurisdictions; some are non-profit corporations, others are organized as profit making corporations. Funds are raised through donations, sale of stock, private borrowing, or from the Small Business Administration. Most funds are used to construct industrial facilities to the specifications of particular firms; these facilities are then leased to the firms. Funds are also used to make working capital loans, purchase land, construct sites, or purchase leases on an anticipatory basis.

State Industrial Finance Authorities. Started in New Hampshire in 1955, there are now 13 states that have authorized such programs. State authorities either guarantee loans made by private lenders or make direct loans from state funds to industry by issuing industrial development bonds (IDBs).

Proponents of IDBs have pointed out that by exempting interest payments from federal taxable income, the rate of return that must be earned is reduced from 15 percent to 10 percent, allowing expansion into more marginal investments. Stober and Falk (1969) point out that the advantage also includes the fact that the local government that builds the facility faces no corporation income tax, and can thus break even if it only makes enough in receipts to cover interest payments. The lease payments it charges to industry are, therefore, less than

the implicit lease payments a private firm would have to charge itself.

One problem with the variety of loan programs offered by states and localities is that they are usually administered by a variety of agencies, inhibiting cooperation and proliferating confusion. Milwaukee, by contrast, administers three loan programs—for housing rehabilitation, commercial rehabilitation and small business financing—through one super agency, the Department of City Development. The result has been the successful coordination and leverage of public funds.

Questionnaires that have been used to assess the role of IDBs are rarely convincing. In Alabama, one-third of 54 firms using IDB financing claimed they would have located elsewhere without that incentive, but fully ninety percent of eligible firms failed to take advantage of the provision (Alabama Business Research Council, 1970).

Overall, it appears that these loan subsidies are not cost effective development tools. States and local areas would be better off making direct cash grants to businesses—firms would feel as well off with a cash grant that is less than the foregone tax receipts under the present system—although this may not be politically palatable. Perhaps the answer is to concentrate on infrastructure development and new development finance corporations—policies whose benefits are less tied to a few large corporations.

WHAT CAN STATES DO?

The preceding discussion suggests several areas where states can take action or lobby for federal assistance:

■ First, interstate tax competition should be reduced, perhaps with federal assistance.
■ Second, states should act to reduce interjurisdictional tax incentive competition within their own borders.
■ Third, income tax exemption for development financing bond interest payments should be replaced by interest subsidies.
■ Fourth, states should focus on infrastructure development and cutting red tape rather than on tax incentives.
■ Finally, if special incentives are to be used, they should be in the form of broadly applied wage subsidies rather than capital incentives.

Interstate Tax Competition

It is difficult for the individual state to act. Failure to offer tax incentives may well bring cries from local industry. Political opponents will be given a readily available, if ultimately fallacious, platform. The gubernatorial campaigns during the fall of 1978 echoed with cries for tax breaks. It seems clear that federal legislation is needed to make it hard for states to offer these bribes.

Can the federal government help? Outright prohibition is probably impossible, or extremely difficult, on constitutional grounds. There are, however, some measures that could be implemented:[11]

■ Overall Economic Development Plans prepared by states and municipalities that offer special incentives could be rejected by EDA on the grounds that they fail to treat all companies equally. This would make those areas ineligible for Title II loan guarantees, and, perhaps, for Title IX grants.
■ HUD could reject community development plans on the same grounds, and hold up CDBG and UDAG funds.
■ General Revenue Sharing funds could be reduced for each dollar of local taxes foregone through an exemption or abatement program that did not apply uniformly to all firms.
■ The corporation income tax code could include a federal tax penalty on firms granted special local tax exemptions.

It is difficult to assess the effectiveness of an initiative of this sort. State and local governments may substitute direct expenditures on infrastructure and business services in order to attract businesses. Reduced tax expenditures may influence economic development patterns.

Success depends on how broadly the anti-tax provisions are applied, and how much effort is devoted to enforcing them. Experience with hastily implemented countercyclical programs suggests that local governments can avoid ill-defined and loosely enforced federal regulations (Vernez and Vaughan, 1978). On the other hand, threat of withdrawal of education grants has been used, with some success, to encourage the integration of schools and the provision of special school services. Without a careful review of the relationship between federal enforcement activity and state and local behavior, and more details on how the program would be enforced, it is difficult to predict the outcome. Generally, states should rely less on firm-specific special incentives and more on actions that improve the overall business climate.

States should also rely more on across the board tax cuts and infrastructure development in order to attract industry. Most of these tax cuts should be directed at personal rather than business taxes, in response to taxpayer unrest.

Interjurisdictional Tax Competition

States have considerable control over how their component jurisdictions shape their taxes to attract industry. Again, the most important measures are those that redistribute resources among jurisdictions (Chapter 4), but states could also penalize areas that step out of line in an aggressive tax incentive program.

Exemption of Local Municipal and Development Bonds from Income Tax States can do little to reduce reliance on local bond tax exemption, except through outright prohibition. If local public sector borrowing is to be made easier and cheaper, then states must appeal to the federal government to allow the issuing of taxable bonds which are eligible for a federal interest rate subsidy.

Given the prevailing atmosphere of fiscal restraint, it is reasonable to anticipate that an interest subsidy rate of 33-35 percent is politically feasible since this would involve little net increase in Treasury outlays and yet would provide state and local governments with substantial benefits. A report to the House Ways and Means Committee in 1976 estimated that a 35 percent subsidy would, in the long run, save state and local governments about $1.0 billion a year, and cost the Treasury only $140 million annually.

The shift into the taxable market will have a small effect on interest rates—an increase of between 0.01 and 0.03 on corporate rates (*Fortune,* 1973). Table 20 shows benefits of a $1 billion reduction in borrowing costs, both per capita and per $1000 of personal income, by state, and is based on the simplifying assumption that benefits are distributed among states according to their share of total state and local debt. States are grouped according to their fiscal "blood pressure" as calculated by the Advisory Commission on Intergovernmental Relations. It is apparent that benefits would be greatest in fiscally distressed states, states which tend to be located in the Northeast.

The targeting is not precise, however. Among the "low blood pressure" areas receiving high benefits are Alaska, Nebraska, and the District of Columbia. California and the New England states receive little assistance among the "high and rising" states. Actually, the benefits would be more effectively targeted toward fiscal distress than the table suggests. The taxable option will be exercised most readily by those distressed states and cities in the Northeast whose relatively low bond rating has either squeezed them out of the bond market or has left them paying very high rates. The proportional federal subsidy would mean that their subsidy per $1 million of bonds issued would be much higher than elsewhere. The broader market for taxable bonds will also lead to a reduction in the net interest rate they would have paid had they stayed in the tax exempt market, and reduce fluctuations.

The program has several desirable outcomes: it helps fiscally distressed areas; it encourages increased public borrowing at a time when lack of capital spending is viewed by some as nearing a crisis; it is **107**

Table 20
Fiscal Blood Pressure and Benefits Per Capita and Per $1000 of Personal Income of a $1 Billion Reduction in State and Local Borrowing Costs

High and Falling	per p.c.	$1000	High and Rising	per p.c.	$1000
Wisconsin	3.3	.54	New York	10.0	1.41
Arizona	4.8	.84	Vermont	4.9	.91
New Mexico	2.9	.55	Massachusetts	6.1	.92
Louisiana	4.9	.94	California	3.7	.53
Wyoming	4.5	.70	Hawaii	7.9	1.13
Montana	2.7	.48	Minnesota	5.0	.81
Oregon	6.7	1.09	Maine	3.7	.70
Washington	8.9	1.33	Nevada	4.4	.64
Mississippi	3.1	.69	Maryland	6.0	.88
Unweighted Average	*4.6*	*.79*	Rhode Island	4.6	.74
			West Virginia	4.0	.76
			Michigan	4.0	.59
			Michigan	4.0	.59
			New Jersey	4.7	.64
Low and Falling	per p.c.	$1000	Delaware	7.7	1.09
			Pennsylvania	5.5	.85
South Dakota	2.0	.40	*Unweighted Average*	*5.4*	*.82*
Iowa	1.9	.31			
Colorado	3.3	.51			
Utah	2.1	.41			
North Dakota	2.5	.43			
Indiana	2.0	.33	**Low and Rising**		
Idaho	1.3	.24		per p.c.	$1000
Kansas	3.8	.59			
North Carolina	1.9	.35	Kentucky	4.8	.89
Nebraska	7.8	1.30	Connecticut	6.4	.86
South Carolina	3.1	.61	Alaska	21.9	2.24
Texas	4.0	.66	Georgia	3.2	.59
Oklahoma	3.1	.55	New Hampshire	3.3	.57
Florida	3.7	.62	District of Columbia	14.3	1.74
Tennessee	4.3	.82	Virginia	3.3	.52
Alabama	3.3	.65	Missouri	2.5	.42
Arkansas	2.1	.44	Ohio	3.2	.51
Unweighted Average	*3.1*	*.54*	*Unweighted Average*	*7.0*	*.93*

SOURCE: States listed in descending order of "Blood Pressure" in each category, from Advisory Commission on Intergovernmental Relations," *Measuring the Fiscal Blood Pressure of the States—1964-1975,* M-111, Washington, D.C., February 1977; and Bureau of the Census, *Governmental Finances, 1976-1977,* U.S. Department of Commerce, Washington, D.C., November, 1978. The calculations assume that the benefits of the $1 billion savings are distributed in proportion to the states' share of total state local indebtedness.

paid for by the relatively affluent; and will tend, in aggregate, to shift spending toward the less affluent.

Infrastructure Development and Red Tape Cutting

States have typically packaged tax and financial incentives with infrastructure development. Loans and loan guarantee offers are normally packaged together with considerable public investments in necessary infrastructure.

To attract Volkswagen to Pennsylvania, the auto manufacturer was offered not only a low interest $200 million loan, but also a promise to complete construction on railroads and highways leading to the New Stanton site. Ohio gave Honda grants totaling $2.5 million to help finance the building of rail spurs and publicly-owned water and sewer facilities, and even provided CETA funds to cover employee training costs.[12]

A major advantage of developing local infrastructure rather than offering specific tax incentives is that many firms can benefit from better roads, sewers, water supply, and fire and police protection. Such benefits need not be limited to a few large firms. The state, with its superior resources, can step in and help local communities with their development problems.

The state of Massachusetts, in cooperation with local governments, approached the problem of decaying mill towns by recycling old mills and buildings into housing, shopping centers, and recreational facilities.[13]

There are other alternatives to tax incentives. "City officials here think that businesses want good parking, clean neighborhoods and decent land—not gimmicks," claims William Schneider, Executive Director of the City-Wide Development Corporation in Dayton, Ohio.[14] Tax incentives cannot address the roots of the problems that lead to slow growth and rising unemployment. Infrastructure development (or redevelopment) can.

A major barrier to the effective use of "place enhancing" programs to spur local development is the artificial barrier between "economic development" and "community development" programs. This distinction is fostered, at the federal level, by the separation, and lack of coordination, between HUD's community development focus and EDA's emphasis on economic development, although the types of projects financed by each are quite similar. Planning activities for these programs at the state and local level are often undertaken by separate agencies.[15] These agencies seldom interact.

A second barrier to a coordinated "packaging" approach to solving development problems is the ambivalent role of state governments. While states have primary responsibility for planning and distributing funds for highways and water treatment, and partial responsibility for

EDA regular projects and CETA, local jurisdictions have a major share of LPW, CDBG, and parts of CETA. This approach to fund distribution by the federal government impedes coordinated local development efforts. States would do well to rationalize local development efforts by clearly delineating state and local responsibilities. However, the major responsibility must lay with the federal government, and at present, reorganization efforts seem to have been abandoned.

Thus we must conclude that a packaged infrastructure building approach to local economic development has the most promise, but also that there are significant institutional barriers that prevent the realization of its full potential.

Wage Subsidies[16]

Incentives could be used to create jobs by reducing the cost of hiring additional labor. We have argued that payroll taxes have raised the cost of labor —particularly unskilled labor—and have contributed toward the problem of unemployment. The number of jobs available would increase if this cost were reduced.[17]

A wage subsidizing incentive could take several forms. The simplest form would be modelled on the investment tax credit, and allow a tax deduction for any increase in the firm's payroll. Thus if its payroll increases by $10,000 in a year, the firm may deduct, say, $1,000 from its taxable income. This is analogous to the federal employment tax credit adopted in 1977. This measure naturally provides most of its assistance to growing areas where employment would be expanding anyway, and does little to focus on the hard-to-employ. The new Targeted Jobs Tax Credit is applicable only to the hard-to-employ, and can be taken as a credit as well as a reduction in taxes. It meets many of these objectives. An alternative would be to provide employment vouchers to unemployed individuals, based upon their past income and unemployment experience. An employer could redeem these vouchers—either for cash or reduced payroll taxes—for each week that they provided the worker with a job. The cash value, or subsidy, would decline over time as the subsidized worker gained work experience.

Consider a simple numerical example. Someone unemployed more than thirty weeks and with a household income of less than $6000 in the previous year could present an employer with vouchers worth $75 per week, a subsidy that would slowly decline to zero over a 24 month period. He or she would compete—presumably for unskilled jobs—in the labor market and could secure a job paying close to the minimum wage—$116 for a forty hour week. The employer would be reimbursed for most of the wage costs. If the worker were employed for a full year, the employer would receive tax subsidies of $2808 toward a wage bill of $6032. During the second year, the subsidy would fall to $1078.

The program has the advantage of actually increasing the number of jobs available, and in targeting those jobs to the needy. The recently passed targeted jobs tax credit offers federal subsidies of about $1700 for employers hiring eligible workers. States could add to the program, offering reduced payroll or property taxes, and using CETA funds to cover part of the program cost.

A potential disadvantage of a wage subsidy is that employers might fire an employee as soon as the subsidy was reduced to hire a more subsidized worker. This objection is more apparent that real. First, there need be no sudden cut-off of the subsidy. Second, hiring and firing involves costs to the employer. And third, there would be an increase in the number of jobs available. The policy merits much deeper consideration than it has received in the past.

FOOTNOTES TO CHAPTER 6

1. Logically, reducing the death rate of firms could also boost local growth, but death rates do not vary much among areas, and seem fairly intractable to local policies.

2. These slogans were described in a column by James Sterba in the *New York Times,* July 18, 1978.

3. The exceptions are Alabama, Minnesota, and Tennessee.

4. Bird, 1966, parts I and II; Bridges, 1965; Due, 1961; Hellman, Wassall, and Falk, 1976; Hodge, 1979; Gurwitz, 1977; Harrison and Kanter, 1976 and 1978; Morgan and Hackbart, 1974; Mulkey and Dillman, 1976; and Williams, 1967.

5. Quoted in Jerry Jacobs, "Battling for Business," *People and Taxes,* September 1978, p. 9.

6. Some studies have found tax incentives to be cost effective from the viewpoint of local governments. These have tended to ignore the secondary impacts of development, such as population growth. See, for example, Moes (1941); Rinehart (1963); and Sazama (1970).

7. These problems are not present, of course, with property tax incentives, since property taxes must be paid whatever the level of profit of the firm.

8. The concentration of non-taxpaying firms is likely to be greatest in distressed areas, precisely where the stimulus is most needed.

9. Many of these topics are covered in other volumes in this series.

10. Section 107 of the Revenue and Expenditure Control Act of 1968 denies federal tax exemption to industrial development bond issues exceeding $5 million. Such issues fell sharply from $1.6 billion in 1968 to $0.5 billion by 1978. But bonds for water treatment were exempt from the $5 million limit, and by 1976, $4.5 billion in water treatment bonds were issued.

11. For a fuller discussion, see Vaughan (1979).

12. See Cornia, Testa, and Stocker (1978) and Haskins (1977).

13. See Neal R. Pierce, "States as City Savers," *The Washington Post,* 10/11/77.

14. Quoted in "Ailing Cities Spread the Welcome Mat for Business," *U.S. News and World Report,* 12/19/77, p. 76.

15. HUD encourages local jurisdictions to finance planning from CDBG funds (to replace the old 701 planning grants), while EDA is experimenting with developing local planning capacity through 302 planning grants to states and local jurisdictions.

16. Wage subsidies have been recommended by several authors. See Orcutt, who advocated a scheme similar to the one outlined here in an unpublished paper. A more extensive plan has been devised by Bishop (1977). Lester Thurow recently argued the case in the *New York Times,* 1/10/78. See also Roger Vaughan, "Jobs for the Urban Unemployed," in Bryce (1978).

17. Several studies have attempted to measure the elasticity of demand for labor—the percentage increase in the number of employees demanded in response to a given percentage reduction in the cost.

WHAT SHOULD STATES DO ABOUT PERSONAL TAXES?

State economic development programs have traditionally focused upon business taxes. However, there is growing evidence that state differences in personal taxes, especially income and property taxes, may be a more powerful, if indirect, influence on growth than differences in business taxes.

The burden of state and local taxes is a composite of a number of taxes. The most important are personal income taxes, property taxes, and sales taxes. In 1977, personal income, property, and sales taxes accounted for over $123 billion—out of $175 billion in total state/local tax revenues (Table 21).[1] Other sources of revenue from households include state-operated gambling operations and fees and charges.

Within this broad total, there are wide variations among states (Table 22). Oregon, Massachusetts, Montana, Alaska, New York, and Wisconsin rely on the personal income tax for at least 40 percent of their total revenues. Louisiana, Maine, Mississippi, New Mexico, and Ohio raise less than 15 percent of their revenue from personal income taxation. Connecticut, Florida, Nevada, South Dakota, Texas, and Washington have no income tax. The result is that per capita revenues in 1977 ranged from $59 in Louisiana to $400 in New York. Residents of some cities also face personal income taxes.[2]

Residential property taxes also vary sharply among states.[3] In 1975, Massachusetts topped all other states, collecting $229 per capita, followed by New Jersey $216, California $202, and Connecticut $199 (Table 22). At the other end of the scale, Alabama collected only $22 per capita, Lousiana $32, Kentucky $37, and Mississippi $38.

Sales taxes range from 7 percent in Connecticut and 6 percent in Pennsylvania and Rhode Island, to only 2 percent in Oklahoma (Table 22). However, many local jurisdictions impose additional sales taxes, so that the rate in New York City is 8 percent, split evenly between state and city. Per capita revenues range from only $65 in Vermont, to $347 in Washington.

Fees, charges and miscellaneous are also a major source of state/local revenue. This category includes everything from inheritance taxes and state gambling revenues to charges for water supply and local tennis courts. Finally, the growing difficulty of increasing tax revenues from regular sources has broken down the traditional moral opposition to gambling. Today, only 5 states (Hawaii, Missouri, Mississippi, Texas, and Utah) ban all forms of gambling. In many **113** states, publicly-run gambling—from casinos and sports betting to parimutuel horse racing and lotteries—are operated as a source of revenue.

Through state organized gambling, the state can create a good or service which is strongly in demand—or at least take over its production from illegal enterprises—and tax it. Only those that wish to gamble need pay the tax. Atlantic City has tried to create a "Las Vegas East" to revive its flagging tourist trade and raise revenues. Mayor Koch of New York City has even proposed—only half tongue in cheek—that the city run a numbers game. It is a politically expedient move.

New Hampshire introduced the first lottery in 1963, and by FY 1973, eight states were operating lotteries (Table 23). But lotteries are, at best, a marginal source of revenue.

EFFICIENCY

The evidence suggests that the collection of this burden of state and local taxes has several efficiency costs:

Table 21
State and Local Revenues from Personal Income Taxes and Property Taxes, Selected Years

Tax	Tax Revenues ($ Millions)			
	1960	1965	1970	1977
Personal Income Taxes	2,536	4,417	12,114	29,245
States	2,282	3,947	9,583	25,493
Localities	254	470	1,531	3,752
Property Taxes	16,238	23,187	36,546	62,335
States	520	657	923	2,260
Localities	15,718	22,530	35,623	60,275
General Sales Taxes				
States	4,302	6,711	14,177	30,896
Localities	1,339	2,059	3,068	5,417

SOURCES: *Survey of Current Business,* May 1978; Bureau of the Census, *Governmental Finances, 1976-77,* Washington, D.C., various years.

Income Tax

■ Interstate differences have encouraged the migration of some high income households toward lower taxing states. However, the effect may not be strong and the quality of the research has been relatively weak.

■ High income tax rates tend to be capitalized in high wages, especially among the more mobile labor force groups.

■ Income taxes discourage labor force participation.

Property Taxes

■ High local property taxes used for redistributive programs have encouraged more affluent households to move away from central cities into relatively homogeneous suburban jurisdictions.

■ Fear of reassessment has not been a major deterrent in property rehabilitation decisions, but high rates do discourage investment by depressing values.

Sales Tax

■ High local rates lead to a loss of local retail sales and retail employment.

Fees and Charges

■ Fees and charges may be used to increase efficiency in the use of public services.

Income Tax

It is difficult to prove that local income tax rates influence residential location. High rates can be accompanied by high quality public services that attract migrants. Some evidence does suggest that high tax rates deter net inmigration and affluent households more than low income households, thus leading to a growing concentration of the poor in high taxing locales. But such data are often highly aggregated, and few studies have considered the quality of local public services. There is room for considerable doubt. One reason why personal income taxes may not influence decisions as much as some critics contend is that, for high income households that itemize their federal returns, local taxes are deductible. Thus for these households the burden is reduced by up to 50 percent.

Migrants are sensitive to cost of living differentials in their choice of destination, and local taxes may contribute significantly to these differentials. A number of studies have found that an increase in local taxes per capita of about one percent would have little or no impact on black inmigration in a metropolitan area and might reduce the rate of white inmigration by about 0.3 percent.[4] However, Liu (1977) found the state tax rate had little effect on migration decisions.

Table 22
Characteristics of State/Local Personal Taxes, 1977

State	Personal Income Tax Rate as Percent of Household Income[1] 5,000	15,000	25,000	Personal Income Tax Per Capital Revenue	Personal Income Tax Share of State/Local Revenue	Property Tax (1975) Per Capita Revenue	Property Tax (1975) Share of State/Local Revenue	General Sales Tax Rate	General Sales Tax Per Capita Revenue	General Sales Tax Share of State/Local Revenue	Charges and Miscellaneous Per Capita Revenue	Charges and Miscellaneous Share of State/Local Revenue
Alabama	0.3%	1.5%	2.3%	96.8	13.2	22	8.1%	4	160.4	21.9	225.5	30.8
Alaska	—	1.6	2.5	615.3	20.4	79	44.5	—	78.5	2.6	679.8	22.5
Arizona	0.6	1.3	2.5	105.4	10.2	106	30.7	4	263.6	25.6	206.6	20.0
Arkansas	—	1.7	2.9	110.0	16.3	35	16.6	3	131.0	19.4	169.9	25.2
California	-0.7	1.1	2.5	240.3	18.2	202	34.7	4¾	239.4	18.1	230.8	17.5
Colorado	-0.5	1.1	2.6	161.3	14.7	97	28.7	3	216.9	19.7	271.6	24.7
Connecticut	—	—	—	84.2	8.0	199	39.3	7	188.2	17.9	166.1	15.8
Delaware	0.8	2.7	4.7	344.5	31.6	53	11.9	—	—	—	287.2	26.3
D.C.	-0.1	2.8	4.6	366.6	30.2	102	19.5	5	201.6	16.6	158.7	13.1
Florida	—	—	—	22.8	2.7	82	24.5	4	164.5	19.2	232.6	27.1
Georgia	—	1.2	2.7	133.3	15.9	72	22.8	3	154.7	18.4	225.7	26.9
Hawaii	-3.4	2.6	4.3	256.2	20.7	86	13.4	4	378.9	30.6	269.3	21.8
Idaho	-1.2	1.8	3.6	159.4	20.2	51	24.7	3	115.4	14.6	182.0	23.0
Illinois	0.5	1.8	2.1	160.5	15.6	117	31.0	4	200.1	19.4	167.0	16.2
Indiana	1.0	1.7	1.8	113.3	13.3	88	28.6	4	197.3	23.1	197.0	23.1
Iowa	1.1	2.4	3.4	186.0	19.0	87	29.5	3	119.6	12.2	237.2	24.2
Kansas	0.5	1.2	2.0	144.3	14.9	83	31.2	3	147.5	15.2	233.0	24.1
Kentucky	—	2.0	2.9	171.6	22.3	37	14.5	5	132.5	17.3	173.4	22.6
Louisiana	—	0.9	1.0	58.7	6.5	32	11.0	3	207.6	23.0	263.1	29.2
Maine	—	0.7	2.1	100.4	12.6	104	29.5	5	154.3	19.4	146.4	18.4
Maryland	0.6	2.3	3.1	317.2	27.5	126	23.2	5	113.6	9.8	253.6	22.0
Massachusetts	-0.5	3.3	4.0	278.7	23.5	229	41.9	5	77.5	6.5	172.4	14.5
Michigan	-1.6	0.8	1.4	268.4	23.6	130	29.3	4	154.6	13.6	255.7	22.5
Minnesota	-6.9	4.8	6.7	303.8	25.8	103	22.9	4	117.4	10.0	278.4	23.6
Mississippi	—	0.7	1.8	74.0	10.0	38	15.6	5	198.1	26.8	214.0	29.0
Missouri	—	1.0	2.1	121.1	15.7	76	25.0	3⅛	151.7	19.7	204.2	26.5
Montana	1.0	2.2	3.6	171.0	17.9	95	36.0	—	—	—	229.0	23.9
Nebraska	-1.6	1.3	2.1	132.8	13.1	91	34.4	3	138.2	13.7	256.2	25.3

State												
Nevada	—	—	—	49.5	5.8	133	23.4	3	224.0	17.4	192.4	22.7
New Hampshire	—	—	—	—	—	163	47.8	5	125.1	11.1	190.8	17.0
New Jersey	—	1.5	1.7	142.8	12.7	216	41.7	3¾	222.5	23.6	324.6	34.4
New Mexico	-2.8	0.1	1.4	46.8	5.0	34	11.9	4	218.9	14.2	288.3	18.7
New York	—	2.4	4.4	399.9	25.9	181	29.1	3	118.2	15.7	155.5	20.7
North Carolina	0.8	2.5	3.9	179.3	23.9	48	17.2	3	157.4	16.1	342.0	35.0
North Dakota	—	1.1	3.1	109.7	11.2	54	21.3	4	112.5	13.3	203.1	24.1
Ohio	0.2	0.8	1.5	138.7	16.4	86	29.6	2	—	—	235.4	28.2
Oklahoma	0.1	0.6	1.8	102.7	12.3	41	16.2	—	—	—	—	—
Oregon	0.7	2.8	4.3	272.1	25.1	128	32.3	6	121.9	14.6	297.5	27.5
Pennsylvania	—	2.0	2.0	220.5	24.0	62	21.9	6	129.2	14.1	149.0	16.2
Rhode Island	—	1.6	2.1	160.7	15.7	150	33.3	4	157.6	15.4	197.0	19.3
South Carolina	0.5	1.7	3.3	136.9	18.3	42	17.0	4	143.2	19.1	204.0	27.3
South Dakota	—	—	—	3.6	0.4	80	35.2	4½	159.1	18.5	239.9	27.9
Tennessee	—	—	—	—	—	52	19.0	4	216.1	29.0	179.5	24.1
Texas	—	—	—	41.5	5.6	68	27.3	4	156.0	18.3	216.1	25.3
Utah	0.4	2.1	3.4	140.8	16.7	65	22.1	3	205.3	24.4	206.5	24.5
Vermont	-0.6	2.3	3.1	177.4	17.9	137	32.8	3	65.0	6.7	190.0	19.5
Virginia	0.5	2.1	3.1	171.2	19.8	83	22.6	4.6	112.2	13.0	185.3	21.4
Washington	—	—	—	—	—	123	22.8	3	347.3	31.3	296.8	26.8
West Virginia	0.9	1.3	1.9	98.9	13.1	39	14.5	3	235.5	31.1	148.4	19.6
Wisconsin	-4.8	3.7	5.6	297.0	27.5	115	27.4	4	142.1	13.2	218.9	20.3
Wyoming	—	—	—	—	—	66	29.4	3	261.8	18.8	387.0	27.8

1. "Effective rates" are computed as the percentage that tax liability is of adjusted gross income (i.e., income after business deductions but before personal exemptions and other allowable deductions). In computing income taxes, it was assumed that all income was from wages and salaries and earned by one spouse. In computing the state income taxes for the $5,000 class, the optional standard deductions, low income allowances, and optional tax tables were used. For the other income classes (based on deductions claimed on federal income tax returns) the following estimated itemized deductions were assumed: $15,000—$3,830; and $25,000—$5,115. For federal tax computations, the zero bracket amount ($3,200) and the earned income credit applied for the $5,000 class; the zero bracket amount for the $15,000 class. For the remaining class, the following estimated itemized deduction was assumed: $25,000—$5,850; (state itemized deductions with the addition of est. state income taxes and less certain deductions not allowed under federal law). Excludes the following states with limited personal income taxes: Connecticut (capital gains and dividends); New Hampshire and Tennessee (interest and dividends).

SOURCE: Advisory Commission on Intergovernmental Relations, *Family Tax Burdens Compared Among States and Cities*, Washington, D.C., 1978; U.S. Bureau of the Census, *Governmental Finances*, various years, Washington, D.C.; "Tax Wealth in Fifty States," *State Government News*, July 1978.

Table 23
State Lotteries in FY 1973

State	Sales ($ Million)	Sales ($ / Capita)	Admini- stration Costs* ($ Million)	Revenue to State ($ Million)	Percent of States Own Revenues	Prizes
New Hampshire	6.8	9.28	1.2	2.6	0.9	3.0
New York	130.0	7.13	16.2	61.8	0.7	52.0
New Jersey	112.7	15.72	10.2	50.7	1.9	51.8
Connecticut	34.7	11.45	4.6	14.5	1.2	15.6
Pennsylvania	124.4	10.55	12.5	57.5	1.2	54.4
Massachusetts	70.6	12.55	7.9	32.1	1.5	30.5
Michigan	135.7	15.29	12.4	62.2	1.5	61.0
Maryland	40.1	10.22	8.0	16.0	1.0	16.0

SOURCE: Roger E. Brinner and Charles T. Clotfelter, "An Economic Appraisal of State Lotteries," *National Tax Journal*, Vol. XXVIII, No. 4, 1975, p. 396.

*Operating costs, agents' fees and bank fees on other revenues.

Tax differentials are capitalized in wage differentials, although only among the mobile, affluent occupations.[5] Skilled workers who operate in a regionwide, nationwide, or even international labor market demand, and receive, higher wages and salaries for living in high taxing locales. In fact, this may lead to greater interarea cost differentials than do business taxes.

The view that low personal income taxes are an incentive for economic development is well expressed by a Houston Chamber of Commerce official who pointed out that: "Houston has not found the need to stimulate the economy artificially by the granting of special tax moratoriums on property taxes or the offering of industrial bonds through special economic development corporations. The major tax incentive is the lack of a state or local income tax."[6] A similar view is expressed by a businessman who moved his operation from New York to Texas: "I can bring in an executive and he will get a 20 percent boost in income after expenses at the salary he earned elsewhere."[7]

The Advisory Commission on Intergovernmental Relations (1978) concluded that:

> The great variation in state use of the personal income tax stands out as the most potentially harmful tax differential in our federal system. There is little prospect in the near future for a substantial reduction in the great variations in state personal income tax burdens unless: (A)

the federal government provides special help to the high income tax states thereby enabling them to cut their income tax rules, and/or (B) takes coercive action to encourage non-income tax states and low income tax states to make more effective use of this revenue source.

Property Tax In 1956, Charles Tiebout outlined what emerged as the dominant view regarding the effects of interjurisdictional differences in taxes and services in residential location: "Given . . . . local revenue and expenditure patterns, the consumer-voter moves to that community whose . . . menu of taxes and services best satisfies his set of preferences." The result is a tendency for metropolitan areas and labor markets to fragment into many jurisdictions, each serving a relatively homogeneous population. Population and property values decline in those areas not offering an attractive mix of services at competitive tax prices.

Models derived from the Tiebout hypothesis have been used to analyze patterns of residential location among political jurisdictions in metropolitan areas, and the effect of local public sector activities on local property values.

Different types of households respond differently to local government behavior. Although local government behavior has not significantly influenced the number of households moving to the suburbs, it has contributed to the growing socio-economic segregation between central city and suburbs.

Mayo (1971, 1972) examined the role of four municipal fiscal practices on residential choice: total per capita public expenditures, per pupil education expenditures, school and property taxes, and proportion of the municipal budget allocated to schools, recreation, highways, police, and fire. He found that, "the influence of . . . public services and taxes . . . probably canot be considered a major locational factor (p. 237), "although definitive test of the hypothesis must "await the development of better data on (public service) output measures" as well as the "availability of more disaggregated tax data."[8]

However, differences in public sector activities have contributed to the concentration of low income households in central city jurisdictions. Higher income households frequently move to the suburbs seeking to live among others of similar income, in order to minimize the taxes they must pay for redistributive services for the poor, while the poor are attracted to high taxing locales to take advantage of the implicit transfers (Aaronson and Schwartz, 1973; and Bradford and Kelejian, 1973). Net fiscal surplus[9] significantly explains household residential choice (Bradford and Kelejian, p. 567.)

This selective suburbanization results in the fragmentation of municipal jurisdictions and economic segregation (Aaronson and Schwartz 1973). There is little evidence, however, that suburbs are able to main- ***119*** tain their homogeneity. There is considerable heterogeneity with respect to income among suburban towns, although there is some volitional sorting with respect to education and occupation (Pack and Pack, 1977).

Both the level of property taxes and the quality of the public services affect property values and property investment. Evidence generally indicates that *an increase in taxes leads to a decline in property values, while an increase in the level of public services tends to raise property values* (Oates, 1969). The extent to which changes in local taxes or services are capitalized in property values determines the incidence of the property tax and has important implications for the housing stock and the residential location choices of households. For example, that part of the property tax that operates as an excise tax on housing causes families to buy less. Similarly, real estate developers react to the reduction in the after tax return on investment resulting from a property tax increase by reallocating their capital into alternative investments.

Several studies have found that interarea tax differences, and increases in tax rates over time, are reflected in property values and rents (King, 1973; Mayo, 1973; Smith and Dayak, 1975). King, for example, concludes by distinguishing formal and informal variations in the property tax and by suggesting several circumstances that may determine the extent of tax capitalization in a locale. "The extent of capitalization [would seem to be] critically dependent on the visibility and certainty of tax variations. When differentials arise mostly from assessment vagaries, capitalization is unlikely; but when tax changes occur which are more-or-less uniform and highly visible to potential buyers, capitalization seems probable (p. 96)."

Perhaps the strongest evidence for capitalization comes from studies that have drawn on natural experiments. Wicks, Little, and Beck (1968) tested for changes in market values of homes in a Montana municipality before and after a change in the effective property tax rate. They observed that a $1 increase in a tax bill appeared to reduce sales price by roughly $19, indicating capitalization at a rate of 19:1. Moody (1973) studied the effects of tax changes in the San Francisco area using a fortunate natural experiment in 1962, where residents of San Francisco and its surrounding counties voted whether to support BART and incur the increased property taxes it would require. Although San Francisco opted to participate while neighboring San Mateo County did not, a previously planned transit stop in the border of San Francisco and San Mateo's Daly City was installed. The result is that Daly City residents have access to the subway at no cost in property taxes while their San Francisco neighbors bear the cost in a tax increase of $10 to $15, which depressed sales prices by roughly 120 $900. However, not all of the empirical evidence yields indications of capitalization (Daicoff, 1961; and Mayo, 1972).

The degree to which changes in tax rates or in the level of municipal services are capitalized is greater in the short run—when the supply of housing and public services has not fully adjusted to the tax change. In the long run, market response to such differentials may be evidenced mainly in the quantity and quality of the housing stock. The adjustment problem is further compounded by the fact that, as property values shift and as the composition of the local population changes, the menu of local public services offered by a jurisdiction may also undergo adjustment—a response that Tiebout has hypothesized. A local government obviously tends to adapt its services to suit its residents (Edel and Sclar, 1974).

The general view is that property taxes disrupt the operation of the housing market and act as a disincentive to upgrading and new construction as well as acting as a facilitator of downward transition and blight (Peterson et al., 1973):

> Placing a tax on a good must either raise the price consumers pay for the good or lower the profit producers can earn from supplying it. In either case, the imposition of a tax is likely to lead to a lower level of provision of the good in question. If this reasoning is right, an increase in property tax rates may lead directly to a lower supply of new housing or . . . . it may discourage upgrading and rehabilitation of the current stock and accelerate the decision of landlords in low-income areas to abandon their housing altogether (p. 2).

Peterson et al. conducted an extensive study of intraurban variations in effective tax rates and attempted to assess their effects on upward transitional and stable neighborhoods as well as on downward transitional and blighted neighborhoods. The authors noted substantial variation in tax rates between various types of neighborhoods within a given fiscal jurisdiction. For example, property in stable neighborhoods tended to be taxed at a much lower rate than property in blighted neighborhoods. In general, upward transitional neighborhoods enjoyed the lowest tax rates of all.

> Despite the fact that uniform taxation within each city is mandated by law, the neighborhood variation in several cities exceeds the variation in legal rates adopted by different cities. In Chicago and Baltimore, the sample properties in blighted neighborhoods pay property taxes at a rate ten to fifteen times higher than properties in upward transitional neighborhoods. In these cities, the regressivity of the property tax's effective rate structure is due principally to neighborhood bias in assessments (p. 23).

Although fear of reassessment does not appear to act as a deterrent to investment, the high level of taxation is a major factor (Peterson, *121*

1973; and Sternlieb and Burchell, 1973).

Overall, it appears that the property tax is unpopular, inequitable, and deters residential redevelopment.

Since the property tax falls most heavily on housing, relative to other consumer durables and other types of household investments, critics have argued that it leads to too little investment in housing. But the federal income tax strongly favors housing by allowing the deduction of mortgage interest and local property tax from taxable income and by not taxing the imputed rental income of owner occupied housing. There are no studies that compute the net impact of these two countervailing influences, and how they differ according to household income and local property tax rates.

Sales Tax

Sales taxes are used by many large cities and by states as a source of revenue. Central cities have imposed sales taxes to try to take advantage of their position as retail centers. But local differentials in sales tax rates appear to shift retail activity from high taxing to low taxing areas. If suburban centers fail to follow central city sales tax rates, retail trade is diverted away from the central city. Hamovitz (1966) estimated that for each one percentage point increase in the sales tax rate, New York City's retail sales declined by six percent. In a study of 137 metropolitan areas, Mikesell (1970) found that the decline in central city retail sales was between 2 percent and 11 percent in response to one percentage point increase in the central city sales tax rate. The use of the sales tax, especially by local jurisdictions, is therefore limited by the tax rates in competitive retail centers.

Fees and Charges

Economic efficiency is ensured when, in the absence of market imperfections, consumers of a good, or users of a service, pay the marginal cost of providing the good or service. Therefore, local governments can encourage the efficient use of public facilities or services by charging a price equal to the marginal cost. Obviously, there are many public goods for which fees and charges are impossible to apply—how could motorists be charged for the use of street lighting? But there are some services where changes are appropriate. Consider the following cases:

■ Charging for the use of tennis courts ensures that those who really want to play are not crowded out by those who do not value the experience as much.
■ Charging for water use encourages users not to waste publicly-supplied water.
122 ■ Charging new homes the true cost of hooking up to the municipal

sewer and water system discourages sprawling residential development.

To encourage efficiency in this dynamic context, the revenues should provide the producer of the service with a signal as to whether to expand or contract his level of production. For example, if tennis courts remain crowded when players are paying a fee equal to the marginal cost, then additional courts should be provided. If they are vacant, then perhaps the supply should be reduced. Unfortunately, this feedback information is rarely utilized by state and local governments. Receipts become simply part of general revenues rather than an investment indicator.

User fees are a useful source of additional revenue to states and localities trapped by tax limitation statutes. Los Angeles County is proposing a state law for a fire service fee based upon a building's fire risk classification. Scottsdale, Arizona has no public fire protection—the private service operates on a fee—and the costs are relatively low (Ahlbrandt, 1972). The administrative problems of devising a fee schedule are not insuperable (Pollack, 1972). Fire protection expenditures average about 5 percent of local expenditures; therefore, a fee schedule offers some opportunity for relief. Garbage collection— 3 percent of local expenditures—may also be paid for through a fee.

Perhaps the greatest area where the failure to charge fees has had serious efficiency implications is in residential development. Builders of summer homes in Vermont are required to pay only $19 for an electricity hook up, although the cost to the state is $1350 (National League of Cities, 1975). Neal Peirce notes that as a result of Proposition 13, the expanding suburb of Petaluma near San Francisco now charges developers an "impact fee" of $3000 per acre.[10]

Proposing fees and charges usually encounters two objections. They are administratively clumsy, and they penalize the poor (see below). These objections are not always valid, as we shall see.

EQUITY

The equity of personal taxes has been subject to considerable debate. Some of the major conclusions are:

Income Tax
■ Many states have regressive income tax structures.
■ Certain aspects of the income tax structure—standard deductions and certain exemptions—are regressive.

Sales Tax
■ Although the sales tax is basically regressive, the use of exemptions for food and prescription drugs can reduce its regressivity. But these

exemptions are relatively inefficient.

Fees and Charges
■ Although typically argued to be regressive, fees and charges do not necessarily fall heavily on the poor.

The relative equity of property and income taxation has been debated endlessly and cannot be resolved in this paper. However, we can describe, briefly, some of their relative merits, for it does appear that the two taxes are, in some ways, complementary.

Progressivity. The property tax has traditionally been viewed as regressive, while the income tax is, at best, neutral, and may be progressive. Economists have recently taken a less regressive view of the property tax, and a less progressive view of the income tax, because of the many loopholes that high income earners enjoy. There are no definitive studies of relative progressivity.

Ability to Pay. The income tax tends to be favored because income is a measure of an individual's ability to pay, while the value of property is not. The value of property, however, is strongly correlated with a household's normal, or "permanent," income. Taxable income may be artificially low because of certain tax advantages and thus not an accurate reflection of true income.[11] Again, there is no definite answer as to which tax best measures the true ability to pay.

Value of Benefits Received. It has been argued that since the value of local public services received is related to residential location, taxes should be revised on residential property. However, the relationship between the value of real property and the value of services received is no stronger than that between income and services.

Income Tax

Differences in the rate and progressivity of state and local income taxes have influenced economic development. High taxing states, whose taxes often reflect the high level of locally-financed welfare payments, have lost affluent households.

Effective state personal income tax rates for selected, adjusted household incomes are shown in Table 22. For a household earning $15,000 in 1977, state tax burdens varied from almost zero in New Mexico to above 3 percent in Massachusetts, Minnesota, and Wisconsin. For a family earning $25,000, the range was between 1 percent in Louisiana and 1.4 percent in New Mexico, and 6.7 percent in Minnesota and 5.6 in Wisconsin.

Progressivity is, of course, difficult to define. High income individuals are able to take advantage of tax shelters that range from tax free municipal bonds to the differential treatment of capital gains. However, these options are available in almost all states, so that even though the data presented in Table 22 may not measure true interstate progressivity, they do measure differences in the burden to a given household *among* states.

Many states have little progressivity in their income tax structure. Vertical equity could be improved by increasing the progressivity of the rate (see Chapter 4, above).

Another source of vertical inequity is the practice of granting standard deductions from taxable income, rather than tax credits. For a household with a 10 percent marginal state income tax rate, a $1000 personal deduction is worth $100 in reduced state income taxes (and probably about $500 in reduced federal income taxes). To a family with a 2 percent marginal rate, the deduction is worth only $20. Clearly, it would be more equitable to change from a deduction to a flat tax credit of, say, $40, which would be the same for all households.

Horizontal inequity in income tax structure arises because of the special treatment of certain activities, the most glaring being home-ownership. Two households—one renting and one owning its own home—with equal incomes, family size, and housing units, consuming the same public services, will pay very different federal, state, and local taxes. The argument is that this encourages homeownership which is desirable. But it does so at a massive cost in equity. Federal tax expenditures to those fortunate enough to own their own homes, and have high enough incomes to make itemizing worthwhile, at least equal, if not surpass, federal housing assistance to the poor.

A second major inequity is the deduction of state and local taxes from federal taxable income, originally conceived as a way of helping local areas raise taxes. With only 25 percent of households—the relatively well-off—itemizing, this effectively increases the regressivity of local taxes. This deduction also discriminates against the use of fees and charges by local governments.

Property Tax

There is considerable debate as to the regressivity of the property tax, and how it falls on renters. The weight of the evidence suggests that the tax is regressive, and is, for the most part, passed on to renters in the form of higher rents. This regressivity stems from three factors (Grubb and Hoachlander, 1978):

■ The poor spend a much higher share of their income on housing than the more affluent.

■ Expensive houses are assessed at a lower fraction of market value than low-value houses.

■ Jurisdictions with a high concentration of low income households tend to have higher tax rates than more affluent jurisdictions.

There is little doubt that, among personal taxes, the property tax *125* is regarded as the least equitable. In a Gallup poll, only 10 percent of respondents characterized property taxes as the fairest way of financing state and local services, compared with 43 percent for a sales tax and 36 percent for income tax (11 percent "don't know").[12]

Attempts by states and localities to improve the equity of the tax through homestead exemptions are inequitable for the same reason that standard deductions are inequitable for the income tax. The circuit breaker (see Chapter 4 above) is a much more promising avenue for reform.

Sales Tax

Opponents of the sales tax have long argued that its burden falls most heavily upon the poor. Since the poor rarely itemize their federal tax returns, they are unable to offset local sales taxes against federal income taxes. However, special exemptions such as food for home consumption, clothing, and utilities favor the poor, who spend a large share of their income on these necessities (Schaefer, 1969). Of the 44 states with sales taxes, only 22 (plus the District of Columbia), exempt food purchases; 5 exempt clothing; 16 exempt utility payments; and 37 (plus the District of Columbia) exempt prescription drugs. In addition, 7 states allow a credit against state income taxes for food purchased for home consumption. Some states, therefore, have significant opportunities to improve tax equity by extending sales tax exemptions. Also, Hawaii, New Mexico, and South Dakota extend the sales tax to cover professional services, which increases its progressivity since purchase of these services increases with income.

However, exemptions are a relatively inefficient way of helping the poor since all households benefit, although this may be desirable if the policy is to encourage food consumption against expenditures on other goods. An exemption will always be inferior to income tax credits or cash transfers as a way of reducing regressivity.

Fees and Charges

If there is a charge to enter museums or libraries, or an hourly price for the local tennis courts, then the poor will be discouraged from using these facilities. Public facilities also tend to be used more intensively by the poor—more affluent households belong to private tennis clubs and purchase books. Thus, fees are regressive inasmuch as they are collected disproportionately from the poor.

However, this argument applies only to a limited set of charges. Clearly, summer homes are rarely owned by the poor, and development fees will, primarily, fall on homeowners. A charge for water use (through metering) would probably be progressive. It is also possible to make other charges less regressive—such as free use of tennis courts by low-income groups. Charges are highly equitable in that payments are directly related to the volume of public services consumed.

Gambling

The incidence of gambling revenues is regressive. For example, in Massachusetts, those with incomes below $15,000 constituted 86.9 percent of the population but paid an estimated 91.7 percent of the lottery taxes (Brinner and Clotfelter, 1975). However, there is surprisingly little opposition to state gambling on these grounds. This is probably because the alternative is illegal gambling, and the poor gamble in games that are particularly inequitable (e.g., numbers).

WHAT SHOULD STATES DO?

States and localities can take a number of steps to improve the efficiency and equity of household taxes.

Income Tax
■ Replace standard deductions with standard tax credits.
■ Remove the tax incentive for homeownership (or extend equal benefits to renters).
■ Introduce inflation indexing.
■ Simplify the tax structure.
■ Eliminate the deduction of local taxes from federal taxable income.

Property Tax
■ Improve the efficiency of assessment.
■ Introduce circuit breakers (see Chapter 4 above).
■ Shift some of the tax burden from improvements to land (see Chapter 5 above).

Sales Tax
■ States without exemptions on food and prescription drugs should consider introducing them.
■ Some consideration should be given to extending the tax to cover professional services.

Fees and Charges
■ States should analyze their programs to determine whether fees and charges would be appropriate for some functions.

Income Tax

The first two measures are self-explanatory. But implementation must rest upon changes in federal tax laws if states and local areas are to avoid increased administrative costs. Replacing standard deductions with standard tax credits is a simple step, but one to which federal lawmakers have not given much thought. Removing the bias in favor of homeownership is a major political step, and must be viewed as unlikely. The most politically feasible step would be to extend the same privilege to renters, which would preserve vertical inequity while gaining a little horizontal equity.

Inflation Indexing. Although no politician who endorsed inflation would long survive, inflation is not without its advantages to state and local administrators. An 8 percent across the board increase in prices and income increases local tax receipts by a good deal more than 8 percent, allowing programs to be expanded even after paying higher wages and materials costs. In states with progressive tax rates, taxpayers are nudged into tax brackets in which they owe a higher percentage of their income, the real value of standard deductions shrinks, and property prices tend to rise more rapidly than the Consumer Price Index. The Advisory Commission on Intergovernmental Relations estimated that states received an income tax revenue windfall of $1.2 billion in 1978, and by 1982, making certain assumptions about price level and income growth, the bonus could be $11 billion (ACIR, 1979).

A solution to this inflation tax is to index the value of the standard deduction and tax bracket levels to the local consumer price index. Three states have taken steps to do this. In California, tax brackets, credits on personal exemptions, dependence and blindness exemptions, and the standard deduction are raised by 5 percent each year that the increase in the state's CPI exceeds 3 percent. Colorado, the first state to adopt indexing, required the State Assembly to determine the annual inflation factor to index taxes—6 percent in 1978. Arizona indexed for 1978 only.

Indexing may improve the equity of the tax system, although not by a great deal. It may be more useful in acting as a restraint on state budget officers, for it reduces the fiscal bonus that inflation brings.

Deduction of State and Local Taxes from Federal Taxable Income. At present, the federal government foregoes revenues of about $13 billion because of the deduction of state and local taxes from taxable income. This is made up as follows. Non-business state and local taxes (other than property and gasoline taxes) reduced federal income taxes by $8.1 billion in 1977; property taxes on owner-occupied homes reduced income taxes by $4.5 billion; and gasoline taxes reduced taxes by $0.79 billion. This benefit is largely showered on those with incomes high enough to merit itemizing. This should be replaced with an increased grant program to state and local governments so that the benefits can be distributed much more broadly.

Simplifying Collection. There are several ways to improve collection. States can move toward greater uniformity in their definition

of the tax base, and in the special provisions allowed (Shannon,

1976c). This would involve pushing the federal government to adopt some of the changes recommended in this section. The advantages of simplicity must be weighed against efficiency and equity.

Property Tax   The first question that must be faced is whether the property tax should be maintained as a major source of local revenues. The answer seems to be that it should, providing certain changes are made. A basic advantage with local financing of public services is that it does give households a choice in the level and type of public services they receive. Local governments can reflect local preferences.

Assessment and collection practices need considerable improvement. When the International Association of Assessing Officers surveyed their membership in 1973, more than two-thirds characterized assessing practices as relatively or very poor (Almy, 1973). Property should be reassessed frequently and as scientifically as possible to avoid the wild variations in effective rates that presently exist within a jurisdiction. Several steps need to be taken.

First, data should be computerized to enable assessors to estimate the annual change in value in different *types* of property in different *locations*. Second, a "truth in property taxation" process should be mandated by the state, requiring localities to disclose, as prominently as possible: (1) the tax rate that would yield the same revenues as the previous year; (2) the proposed tax rate; and (3) the expenditure increases that have necessitated revenue increases. A policy of this type has been implemented in Florida and can serve to douse some of the anger that has kindled the taxpayers revolt.

John Shannon (1978) adds five more conditions under which, he feels, the property tax can be maintained and improved as the major source of local revenues.

■ A uniform system for administering the property tax; appraising, by professional appraisers, at market value for all taxable property; state supervision of local appraisers; and full disclosure of assessments.
■ State-financed circuit breakers.
■ Full state assumption of welfare and medicaid benefits, so that residents cannot avoid the burden of redistributive programs by moving across jurisdictional boundaries.
■ An intergovernmental "fair play" policy, so that as a state mandates new programs it helps local authorities bear their cost, and also compensates them for revenue losses resulting from state mandated property tax exemptions.
■ A moderate appetite for public goods and services.

To this list we should add shifting some of the tax burden from **129** improvements onto land, and greater efforts to reduce interjurisdictional fiscal disparities.

Sales Tax

Reducing the regressivity of the sales tax should be high on the agenda of those states that do not have exemptions for food. States should also weigh the benefits of income tax credits as an alternative way of assisting low income households.

FOOTNOTES TO CHAPTER 7

1. Property taxes include business property taxes.

2. The following cities with populations greater than 125,000 impose personal income taxes at these rates:

Akron	1.5%	Lansing Mich.	
Baltimore	50% of State Liability	residents	1%
Birmingham	1%	nonresidents	0.5%
Cincinnati	2%	Louisville	
Cleveland	1%	residents	2.2%
Columbus	1.5%	nonresidents	1.45%
Dayton	.75%	Montgomery	1%
Detroit		Newark	0.5%
residents	2%	New York	from 0.9% to 4.3%
nonresidents	0.5%	Oakland	1%
Flint		Philadelphia	4 5/16%
residents	1%	Pittsburgh (City)	1%
nonresidents	0.5%	Pittsburgh (School District)	1%
Grand Rapids		Portland, Ore.	0.6%
residents	1%	St. Louis	1%
nonresidents	0.5%	San Francisco	1.1%
Kansas City, Mo.	1%	Toledo	1.5%
		Youngstown	1.5%

Source: Commerce Clearing House, *State Tax Guide 1978,* Chicago, 1978.

3. These data are state averages across all jurisdictions.

4. See Cebula (1974 a, and 1974 b); Ostrowsky (1978); and Pack (1973). Elderly migrants (over 65) are seen as relatively insensitive to tax rates (Barsby and Cox, 1965, and Debua, 1974 c).

5. A number of studies have found a positive relationship between taxes and salares. See Izraeli (1973).

6. C ed in ACIR (1978). The right to issue local development bonds has been requested by the Texas Industrial Commission and was subject to a referendum November 1978.

7. Quoted in "Lower Taxes Bring High Employment," *Nation's Business,* October 1976.

8. See also Friedman (1975) and Orr (1975).

9. Net fiscal surplus is defined as the value of local public services received minus the local taxes paid. Differences in the effect of the local public sector according to income are also observed by Mayo (1971 and 1972) and Orr (1975). However, Mayo notes that the influence of educational outlays is "spotty" and confined largely to those with the highest incomes, who tend

to locate in jurisdictions with high educational outlays, usually suburbs (p. 237), a finding reinforced by Friedman's work.

10. Neal R. Peirce, "Proposition 13—A Clamp on Land Use," *Washington Post,* September 15, 1978.

11. Mainly because recent studies have shown that the tax is not shifted completely onto renters, who tend to have lower incomes than homeowners.

12. Cited in "The Big Tax Revolt," *Newsweek,* June 18, 1978. Also, see Shannon (1973).

WHAT SHOULD STATES DO ABOUT THE FISCAL LIMITATION MOVEMENT?

It has been variously described as an earthquake, a landslide, and an avalanche. Constitutional Amendment XIIIA of the California State Constitution was passed on June 6, 1978, the most publicized success of the fiscal limitation movement, and a victory clear enough to have many states and even the federal government thinking twice about taxes and spending (Table 24). John Shannon and Carol Weissert (1978) of the ACIR gave the New York City crisis a 5 on a Richter-like 1 to 10 scale for the state/local finance sector, the 1974-76 recession about 8, and Proposition 13 almost 10. What will be the effects of the movement to limit state and local fiscal behavior? What actions can state governments take? These are the themes of this chapter.

STATE AND LOCAL LIMITATIONS Limitations can either apply to expenditures or tax revenues, state or local governments, and can arise from either state legislation or from constitutional amendment. A combination of common sense and some knowledge of the local fiscal sector would suggest:

■ If the desire, either of the legislature or the voters, is to limit public sector spending, then an expenditure limitation is much more effective and equitable than a tax limitation. The latter does not limit spending and bestows capital gains on property owners.
■ To be effective, a spending limitation must apply to all levels of government, otherwise its main impact will be to shift functional responsibilities to the nonlimited level.
■ Expenditure limitations should be linked to the rate of growth of the local tax base (business and personal income and wealth). Limiting growth to an arbitrary annual percentage is very disruptive during periods of high inflation and local growth.
■ While limitations may encourage efficiency in government—and there is no evidence as yet—they do so at some cost. The flexibility of the government to cope with economic problems is limited, and equity is reduced.
■ Tax limitations that apply only to the tax rate or level of assessment—the most common of all limitations—are rarely effective in

132

Table 24
Proposition 13: Highlights

Property tax rates are limited to 1 per cent of the cash value plus the rate needed to service bond indebtedness approved by the voters before FY 1979. Revenues are collected by each county and apportioned among county governments, municipalities, school districts and special districts in the ratio of their 1978 allocation.

Assessed values will be rolled back to 1975-76 assessment levels and cannot be raised by more than 2 per cent annually unless the property is sold.

Increases in state taxes will require a two thirds majority in both houses of the Legislature, and no new state ad valorem, sales, or transactions taxes on real property is allowed.

Special taxes, except for taxes on real property, can be imposed by local jurisdictions only after approval of two-thirds of the jurisdiction voters.

reducing revenues, since revenues are the product of rates and assessed value. Rate limitations can work if the area practices mandatory 100 percent assessment.

■ Tax revenue limitations of the Proposition 13 type[1] are inequitable and inefficient. While they may express a very real taxpayer grievance, they do not address the problem effectively.

State Tax and Expenditure Limitations[2]

At the time of writing, ten states have some form of actual or intended limitation on their taxing or spending powers. All limitations have been enacted since 1976.

Arizona (1978)	Constitutional	Limits state annual spending to 7 percent of total personal income. Future increases must be approved by two-thirds of both houses.
California (1978)	Constitutional	Any changes in state taxes to increase revenues must be imposed by an act passed by two-thirds of both houses.

133

No new ad valorem taxes on real properties may be imposed.

Colorado (1977)	Statutory	General fund spending may increase by 7 percent, and the reserve fund may be increased by 4 percent. Any surplus revenues must be refunded to taxpayers.
(1978)	Statutory	State personal income tax must be inflation indexed.
Hawaii (1978)	Constitutional	State spending increases are limited by the rate of growth of the local economy. If the general fund exceeds 5 percent of expenditures for two years, taxpayers are refunded.
Illinois (1978)	Non-binding Proposition	Voters approved the proposition that the state should limit state and local spending. No limit yet set.
Michigan (1977)	Statutory	Amounts of over 2 percent of adjusted personal income are deposited in a state stabilization fund and can be withdrawn as personal income declines.
(1978)	Constitutional	State spending increase is limited to the rate of increase in gross personal income.
New Jersey (1976)	Statutory	Spending increase is limited to the increase in state personal income (between 9 and 10 percent in 1978).
North Dakota (1978)	Statutory	State income tax is to be reduced by increasing the amount of income subject to graduated rates.

| Tennessee (1978) | Constitutional | Spending increase limited to the growth of the economy (11 percent in 1978). |

Local Expenditure Limitations   Arizona has had a constitutional limit on the growth of local expenditure of 10 percent since 1921. Booming growth and rising prices have necessitated a number of by-pass tactics, with the endorsement of the state legislature.[3] For example, school expenditures are excluded, as are expenditures of federal monies. Localities can also avoid the limit by declaring a fiscal emergency, a practice that is frequently used. The lesson is that limitations that step beyond the boundaries of practicality tend to be eroded. New Jersey has limited local spending since 1976, but has expanded direct state assistance, which mitigates the impact. Texas adopted local spending limits in 1978.

Local Tax Limitations   Local limitations on property tax rates and assessments have arisen because taxpayers resent paying more taxes as a result of rising property values rather than as a result of planned increases in local expenditures. There is a sense that a fiscal variant of Parkinson's Law is at work: Government spending expands to absorb the revenues available. The most logical expression of this is the "truth in taxation" provisions passed in Florida, which allows revenues to increase only enough to meet planned expenditures, and requires local assessors to advertise exactly what spending increases have necessitated the raising of rates or assessments.

A major disadvantage of this approach is that it perpetuates existing inequities in assessments unless special provisions are included to allow these to be redressed.

But tax limitations do not meet these grievances in an efficient or equitable manner.

THE IMPACTS

Full effects of the recent spate of limitations will take years to unravel. They are unlikely to be as disastrous as opponents predict, nor as benign as supporters forecast. Proposition 13 is likely to have the following effects:

■ Property values in California will increase more rapidly than elsewhere.
■ Local governments will seek ways to reduce the costs of public service delivery.
■ The burden of supporting local services will shift from local to state *135*

governments, particularly welfare and education.

■ Capital expenditures will fall as bond issues are cut. Private developers will have to meet more of the costs of development.

■ Some local services will be cut.

■ Federal money will be cut back, and federal income tax receipts will grow.

Property Values

The most pronounced impact will be a rapid increase in property values in California. As C. Lowell Harriss (1978) summarizes:

> Today's owners, in voting essentially permanent reductions in annual property taxes, have enlarged the *net* benefits to be capitalized in valuing real estate. This one-time capital gain . . . absorbs *now* much of the future benefit of the tax cut . . . Future buyers will pay a higher price—higher by enough to offset the tax benefit.

Inflated property values will increase the downpayment necessary to purchase homes, excluding many households from the tax advantages of homeownership.

The lower tax also reduces the cash flow required to hold undeveloped land, encouraging speculative underutilization. The increased property values will also discourage industrial development (an increase of jobs was one of the benefits offered by proponents). But the price of land, as well as the tax rate, are factors considered by business.

The rising value of property over time (it can be reassessed when it changes hands) will swell tax revenues, dampening the restrictive effect on local governments.

Government Efficiency

Local governments will attempt to cut costs. Anaheim Mayor William O. Talley claims that, "It's making us more creative, more innovative than ever before."[4] The city has been processing data for itself and nine neighboring towns, and sharing training facilities for fire and police recruits with the cities of Orange and Garden Grove. Opportunities for shaving costs in this way are limited to a few percentage points at best. In fact, efficiency may be reduced. Expenditures to be cut are the least visible, including research and information dissemination and planning programs that can help reduce costs in the long run. There is also a fear that salary freezes, another immediate threat, will drive out the most productive workers.[5]

Many areas will switch to fees and charges, which could, if properly used, increase efficiency.

State Assumption of Local Responsibilities

The state of California will take over both the full cost and the administration of the

Table 25
Possible Effects of Proposition 13 on Major Federal Programs

Program	Effect
Mass Transit Assistance	To qualify for Section 5 funds from UMTA, assistance from state and local governments to operators must be greater than the average of the previous two years. $50 million out of a total of $120 million is jeopardized. Participation in UMTA capital grants is also in danger if the 20 per cent match cannot be made.
Highway Aid	Federal aid covers between 70 and 90 percent of highway construction and rehabilitation. State projects will not be affected since they are paid for from earmarked state highway user taxes. About half of locally administered outlays come from property taxes which could endanger $200 million in federal aid, but the California state Department of Transportation has indicated it will provide extra funds.
Airport Aid	Some federal aid to general aviation is endangered because local airports do rely on property taxes.
Education	As much as $385 million in federal aid could be lost if local school districts cut back expenditures. If tuition is increased for post-secondary education, federal expenditures in the Basic Education Opportunity Grant program could rise.
CETA	Although CETA Title VI does contain maintenance of effort provisions, it may be possible for local governments to use CETA funds to rehire local workers laid off because of the tax cut. Some of the $80 million used for work experience, public service employment, summer youth and youth employment and demonstration programs could be lost.
Welfare	The elimination of the scheduled cost-of-living increase to AFDC recipients will reduce program costs by an estimated $144 million, and since the federal government pays about half, $71 million of this will accrue to the federal government, although food stamp benefits, 100 percent federally funded, are estimated to rise by $25 million.
General Revenue Sharing	Since there is a lag in data collection, there will be no immediate change in California receipts. If GRS is reauthorized without change in the allocation formula, the reduction in local tax effect would cost California $100 million in GRS funds in FY 1981 or FY 1982.

SOURCE: Adapted from Congressional Budget Office, *Proposition 13: Its Impact on the Nation's Economy, Federal Revenues, and Federal Expenditures,* Congress of the United States, Washington, D.C., July 1978, pp. 17-26.

welfare program, relieving counti. s of an estimated $1.6 billion in expenditures. Cutting welfare was one of the reasons that voters gave for approving the measure. The program is now removed from their direct control. Education is also likely to become an increasing state responsibility. Local limits have made a mockery of post-serrano equalization programs. In one area, state funding to localities will decline. The state financed circuit breaker has become unnecessary, saving the state $643 million annually.

Capital Expenditures

Capital expenditures will decline sharply in California because localities will be unable to offer the necessary "tax base collateral" upon which to issue bonds.[6]

Local Services[7]

Although voters only wanted to cut welfare, and, in fact, favored increasing all other categories of spending, they are likely to experience cuts in several others services—those typically regarded as luxury services by local officials. Summer schools and special services to the handicapped have gone, and arts and recreation programs have been severely affected. The California Arts Council has lost 60 percent of its budget, and the Los Angeles Philharmonic 50 percent.

Federal Taxes and Expenditures

A Congressional Budget Office study (1978a) estimates that Californians will pay an extra $1.3 billion in income taxes because of the reduced local taxes for itemization.[8] Table 25 summarizes what may happen to federal grants to California as a result of reduced matching funds.

WHAT CAN STATES DO?

The success in California has led to tax limitation movements in the other 49 states and the District of Columbia. However, John Shannon (1978) does not see a tidal wave of abatement. He argues that the Californian experience is relatively unique and will be difficult to replicate in many other places. Few states have as large a surplus, as high property tax rates, as high an overall tax burden (40 percent above the national average), or as rapidly growing property values.

The results of the November 1978 elections were ambiguous. Limitations passed in some states but failed elsewhere. Many "single issue" tax cut candidates lost. Polls taken during the election indicated that voters favored spending cuts rather than tax limitations. There will be a few more successful property tax rollbacks in states where values have soared. There will be pressure for spending limits at all levels of government. There will also be pressure for more open fiscal policy deliberations. Public sector employment will not grow as rapidly as in the past. And public accountability will be more rigorously pursued.

But states should not panic. The solution is not an interstate competition to limit taxation. It is the adaptation of state and local policies to the political climate of the 1980s. The policies discussed in the preceding chapters provide a basis upon which states can improve the equity and efficiency of their fiscal practices. The appropriate response is not a mindless "more frugal than thou" stance, but a carefully thought-out reform of the ways taxes are collected and expenditures determined.

FOOTNOTES TO CHAPTER 8

1. Property tax receipts will decline from an estimated $10.3 billion to only $3 billion.

2. Much of the data in this section comes from National Governors' Association, 1978a.

3. See Bruce Koon, "Living with Limits," *Wall Street Journal*, 11/3/78.

4. Quoted in Peter Nye, "What Happened in California," *Nation's Cities*, August 1978.

5. James Ring Adams, "Coping with Proposition 13," *Wall Street Journal*, 10/10/78.

6. Proposition 13 limitations excluded revenues necessary to service existing debts from the 1 percent tax limitation.

7. See Peter Nye, op. cit.; Clint Page, "The Impact of Proposition 13," *Nation's Cities*, August 1978; Stephen J. Sansweet, "Proposition 13's Impact on the Arts," *Wall Street Journal*, 7/14/78; and U.S. Conference of Mayors, *The Taxpayers' Revolt and the Arts*, Washington, D.C. 1978.

8. This is allocated as follows: $490 million from owner occupied residential property (compared with a property tax reduction of $2341 million); $179 million from owners of residential rental property (against a tax savings of $1200 million); 28 million from commercial and industrial property (a tax savings of $1916 million); and $361 million from agriculture ($944 million).

BIBLIOGRAPHY

This paper covers a very broad array of topics. This bibliography allows the interested reader to pursue some of these topics in greater depth. It is organized, broadly, along the major issues covered in the text. Sources that provide a useful summary of each issue are marked with an asterisk.

While there is no single source that provides an overview to all aspects of state and local fiscal behavior, the interested reader may find Maxwell and Aronson's *Financing State and Local Governments,* published by the Brookings Institution in Washington, D.C. (1977), a useful place to start. For an up-to-date discussion of recent changes in fiscal policy and of topical issues, the Advisory Commission on Intergovernmental Relations (ACIR) publishes an annual *Significant Features of Fiscal Federalism.* This, and the many other publications of the Commission, are invaluable sources. Finally, the Municipal Finance Offices Association in Washington, D.C. has published a *Compendium of Current Research on State and Local Finance and Financial Administration,* which contains essays summarizing the state of the art in major areas together with a thorough index and description of ongoing research, which they plan to update regularly. This can put fiscal practitioners in touch with those conducting relevant studies.

Data is a constant problem for those wishing to understand what is happening in the state and local public sector. The U.S. Bureau of the Census in Washington, D.C. conducts a census of state ands local governments every five years. The most recent, in 1977, is not yet published, and thus we rely upon 1972 data. The Census Bureau also publishes a less thorough, but still useful, *Governmental Finances.* The most recent edition, published in the fall of 1978, covers FY 1977. The ACIR also conducts surveys of local governments on relevant issues, and is the source of a great deal of data. Its journal, *Intergovernmental Perspective,* often contains useful summaries of on-going projects. For an up-to-date description of state tax codes and revenues, see the *State Tax Guide,* revised annually by the Commerce Clearing House in Chicago. The Tax Foundation in Washington, D.C., compiles tables on governmental fiscal behavior biennially, in *Facts and Figures in Government Finance.* The next issue is due in the summer of 1979. Economic and demographic data are available in the *Survey of Current Business,* published monthly by the Bureau

of Economic Analysis, U.S. Department of Commerce. One or two issues annually deal with state and local government behavior in a disaggregated manner.

Allocation of Taxable Income
ACIR, 1975; Hellerstein, 1975 and 1977; Cahoon and Brown, 1973.

Assessment and Collection
Almy, 1973; D.C. Tax Revision Commission, 1978; Hellerstein, 1977; Shannon, 1971 and 1977; Stolz and Purdy, 1977.

Circuit Breakers (see Property Tax Relief)

Economic Development
Components of Change: Allaman and Birch, 1975; Birch, 1978; Jusenius and Ledebur, 1976 and 1978; Ledebur, 1978; Wolman, 1978*.
Location Determinants: Burns, 1977; Chinitz, 1960; Dorf and Emerson, 1978; EDA, 1971; Fields, 1976; Fuchs, 1962; Fulton, 1971; Harris and Hopkins, 1972; Huntington and Kahn, 1976; Jones et al., 1975; Kemper, unpublished; Moses and Williamson, 1967; Olvey, 1972; Perloff et al., 1973; Steinnes, 1977; Stone, 1976; Struyk, 1972; Struyk and James, 1975; Thompson, 1965; Vaughan, 1977*; Weinstein and Firestine, 1978; Wheat, 1973.

Exempt Property (see also Incentives)
Hellman and Sifniotis, 1978; Peterson, 1973; Pfister, 1976.

Federal Aid
ACIR (Fiscal Federalism); Barro, 1978.*

Federal Assumption
Barro, 1978; Hamilton and Rabinovitz, forthcoming*.

Fiscal Capacity
ACIR, 1971 and 1977a; Akin, 1973; Barro, 1978; Manvel, 1971.

Fiscal Crises
ACIR, 1973b; Aronson and King, 1978; Barro, 1978.

Gambling
Brinner and Clotfelter, 1975; *Gambling in America,* 1977; Suits, 1978.

Incentives (See also Exempt Property and Taxes and Business Location)
Bird, 1966; Bridges, Parts I and II, 1965; Cornia, Testa, and Stocker, 1978*; Falk et al., no date; Harrison and Kanter, 1976 and 1978; Hellman, Wassall, and Escowitz, 1973; Hellman, Wassall and Falk, 1976; Jack Fawcett Associates, 1976; Moes, 1961; Morgan and Hackbart, 1976; Mulkey and Dillman, 1976; Rinehart, 1963; Ross, 1953; Sazama, 1970; Sherman and Willett, 1969; Stober and Falk, 1967; Surrey, 1970.

141

Incidence (see also Investment, Taxes and Business and Residential Location)
   Business Taxes: Bahl and Shellhammer, 1969; Harberger, 1962; Pechman, 1966; Stockfish, 1961; Vasquez and deSeve, 1977.
   Income Tax: Lile and Soule, 1969; Moscovitz, 1972; Pechman and Okner, 1974*.
   Property Tax (see also Property Values . . .): Aaron, 1975; Arnott and MacKinnon, 1977; Black, 1977; Break, 1975; McClure, 1977*; Mieszkowski, 1972*; Netzer, 1973; Pechman and Okner, 1974; Peterson et al., 1973; Polinsky and Rubinfeld, 1978; Zimmerman, 1973.
   Sales Tax: Schaefer, 1969.

Industrial Development Bonds
   Alabama Research Council, 1970; Jack Fawcett Associates, 1976; Sazama, 1970; Stober and Falk, 1969.

Inflation and Income Taxes
   ACIR, 1976; ACIR, 1979; Greytak and Jump, 1975.

Investment (see also Public Services, Taxes and Business and Household Location)
   Becker, 1969; Beckman, 1974; Hodge, 1979; Peterson, 1973 and 1978*; Sahling, 1978; Sternlieb and Burchell, 1973.

Limitation of Taxes and Expenditures
   Expenditure: ACIR, 1977b; Fuches, 1978; National Governors' Association, 1978b*; Shannon and Weissert, 1978.
   Taxes: ACIR, 1977b; Barkume, 1976; CBO, July and October 1978; Fuchs, 1978; Harriss, 1978; Levy, 1975; National Governors' Association, 1978b*; Neufield, 1977; Shannon and Weissert, 1978.

Municipal Bond Interest Tax Exemption
   Ackerman and Ott, 1970; Fortune, 1973 and 1975; Morris, 1976; Peterson and Galper, 1975; Shaul, 1977*; Vaughan, 1979.

Property Tax Relief
   ABT, 1975; ACIR, 1973a; Bendick, 1976; Cook, 1973; Gold, forthcoming*; Grubb and Hoachlander, 1978; Shannon, 1973.

Property Values, Rentals, and Property Taxes
   Coen and Powell, 1972; Daicoff, 1961; Edel and Sclar, 1974; Hamilton, 1972 and 1973; Heinberg and Oates, 1970 and 1972; Hyman and Pasour, 1973; Moody, 1974; Oates, 1969; Orr, 1968 and 1972; Smith, 1970; Smith and Keyak, 1975; Vaughan and Vogel, 1979*.

Public Services and Residential Location
   Ellickson, 1976; Friedman, 1975; Mayo, 1971 and 1973; Miller and Tabb, 1973; Moody, 1974; Oates, 1969; Orr, 1968 and 1972; Vaughan and Vogel, 1979*.

Resource Taxation
   Gaffney, 1967; Stinson, 1977*; Wead and Koepf, 1976; USDA, 1978.

Revenue Prediction (see also Tax Rate Determinants)
   Auten and Robb, 1976; Bahl and Gretak, 1976*; Greytak and Cupoli, 1978.

Site Value Tax
Archer, 1973; Carlson, 1977; Cuddington, 1978; D.C. Tax Revision Commission,

1978; Finkelstein, 1975; Lindholm, 1977; Lynn, 1977; Oldman and Teachout, 1977; Peterson, 1973 and 1978*; Pollock and Shoup, 1977.

Stabilizing Influence of Taxes
Williams et al., 1973.

State Aid
ACIR, Fiscal Federalism; Barro, 1978; National Governors' Association, 1978a.*

Suburban Exploitation
Bradford and Oates, 1974; Greene, Neenan, and Scott, 1976*.

Taxes and Business Location
Intrastate: Cameron, 1969; Fuller, 1978; Grieson et al., 1977; Hamovitch, 1966; Levin, 1974; Mikesell, 1970; Roniger, 1978; Vaughan, 1977*.
Interstate: Due, 1961; Hodge, 1979; Morgan, 1967; Schmenner, unpublished; Vaughan, 1977*; Williams, 1967.

Taxes and Residential Location
Interstate: Bradford and Kelejian, 1973; Ellickson, 1976; Fuller and Towles, 1977; Hamilton, 1972 and 1973; Heinberg and Oates, 1970 and 1972; James, 1976; Laidler, 1969; Mayo, 1971 and 1973; Vaughan and Vogel, 1979*.
Interstate: Cebula, forthcoming, 1977, 1976, 1974a, b, and c; Greenwood, 1975; Pack, 1973; Vaughan and Vogel, 1979.

Taxes and Wages
Izraeli, 1973.

Tax Base Determinants
Bahl and Greytak, 1976; Barro, 1978*; Booth, 1978; Gerweck and Epp, 1974; Gerard, 1974; Greytak and Cupoli, 1977; Groves and Riew, 1963; Halstead, 1978; Kee, 1968.

Tax Base Sharing
Bahl and Puryear, 1976*; Bahl and Vogt, 1975; Barro, 1978; Fischel, 1976.

Unemployment Insurance
Ehrenberg and Oaxaca, 1976; Feldstein, 1976.

Value Added Tax
Aaron, 1968; ACIR, 1978.

Wage Subsidy
Bishop, 1977; Vaughan in Bryce, 1979.

BIBLIOGRAPHY

Aaronson, J. Richard, and Eli Schwartz, "Financing Public Goods and the Distribution of Population in a System of Local Governments," *National Tax Journal,* Vol. 26, No. 2, June 1973, pp. 137-160.

Aaron, Henry J., *Who Pays the Property Tax: A New View,* Brookings Institution, Washington, D.C. 1975.

———, "Differential Price Effects of a Value Added Tax," *National Tax Journal,* Vol. 21, No. 2, 1968, pp. 162-175.

ABT Associates, *Property Tax Relief Programs for the Elderly,* prepared for U.S. Department of Housing and Urban Development, Washington, D.C., 1975.

Ackerman, Susan, and David Ott, "An Analysis of the Revenue Effects of Proposed Substitutes for Tax Exemption of State and Local Bonds," *National Tax Journal,* Vol. XXIII, No. 4, 1970, pp. 397-406.

Advisory Commission on Intergovernmental Relations, *Intergovernmental Perspective,* Washington, D.C., January 1979.

———, *Differential Economic Growth,* Washington, D.C., 1978a.

———, *Countercyclical Aid and Economic Stabilization,* A-69, Washington, D.C., December 1978 b.

———, *State Mandating of Local Expenditures,* A-67, Washington, D.C., July 1978 c.

———, *The Michigan Single Business Tax,* M-114, Washington, D.C., March 1978d.

———, *Measuring the Fiscal "Blood Pressure" of the States — 1964-1975,* Washington, D.C., 1977a.

———, *State Limitations on Local Taxes and Expenditures,* A-64, Washington, D.C., 1977b.

———, *Inflation and Federal and State Income Taxes,* A-63, Washington, D.C., 1976.

———, *State and Local Doing Business Taxes on Out-of-State Financial Depositors,* report prepared for Committee on Banking, Housing, and Urban Affairs, U.S. Senate, 94th Cong., 1975.

———, *State-Local Finances, Significant Features of Fiscal Federalism,* M-79, Washington, D.C., 1974a.

———, *The Property Tax in a Changing Environment,* Washington, D.C., 1974b.

———, *Financing Schools and Property Relief—A State Responsibility,* A-40, Washington, D.C., January 1973a.

———, *City Financial Emergencies—The Intergovernmental Dimension,* A-42, Washington, D.C., July 1973b.

———, *Measuring the Fiscal Capacity and Effort of State and Local Areas,* M-58, Washington, D.C., March 1971.

———, *Metropolitan Fiscal Disparities,* A-31, Washington, D.C., 1967.

Ahlbrandt, R.S., Jr., "Efficient Output of a Quasi-Public Good-Fire Services," Ph.D. dissertation, University of Washington, 1972.

Akin, John S., "Fiscal Capacity and the Estimation Method of the Advisory Commission on Intergovernmental Relations," *National Tax Journal,* Vol. XXVI, No. 2, 1973, pp. 275-291.

Alabama Business Research Council, *Industrial Development Bond Financing: Business and Community Experiences and Opinions,* University of Alabama Press, 1970.

Allaman, Peter M., and David L. Birch, "Components of Employment Change for States by Industry Group, 1970-72," Joint Center for Urban Studies of M.I.T. and Harvard University, September 1975.

Almy, Richard R., "Rationalizing the Assessment Process," in George E. Peterson, ed., *Property Tax Reform,* The Urban Institute, Washington, D.C., 1973.

Archer, R.W., "Site Value Taxation in Central Business District Redevelopment," The Urban Land Institute, Washington, D.C., 1972.

Arnott, Richard J., and James C. MacKinnon, "The Effects of the Property Tax" A General Equilibrium Simulation," *Journal of Urban Economics,* Vol. 4, 1977, pp. 389-407.

Aronson, J. Richard, and Arthur E. King, "Is There a Fiscal Crisis Outside of New York," *National Tax Journal, Vol. XXIX, No. 4, 1976, pp. 422-435.*

Bahl, Roy W., and David Greytak, "The Response of City Government Revenues to Changes in Employment Structure," *Land Economics,* Vol. 52, Nov. 1976.

Bahl, Roy W., and David Puryear, "Regional Tax Base Sharing: Possibilities and Implications," *National Tax Journal,* Vol. 29, Sept. 1976, pp. 328-335.

Bahl, Roy W., and Kenneth L. Shellhammer, "Evaluating the State Business Tax Structure: An Application of Input-Output Analysis," *National Tax Journal,* Vol. XXII, No. 2, 1969, pp. 203-216.

Bahl, Roy W., and Walter Vogt, *Fiscal Centralization and Tax Burdens,* Ballinger Publication Company, Cambridge, Mass., 1975.

Barkume, Anthony J., "Criteria for Voting Judgments on a Property Tax Initiative: An Analysis of the Watson Amendment," *National Tax Journal,* Vol. XXIX, No. 4, 1976, pp. 448-460.

Barro, Stephen M., *The Urban Impacts of Federal Policies: Vol. 3, Fiscal Conditions,* R-2114-KF/HEW, The Rand Corporation, April 1978.

Becker, Arthur P., *Land and Building Taxes: Their Effects on Economic Development,* Madison, University of Wisconsin Press, 1969.

Beckman, John W., *Industry in New York: A Time of Transition,* The 1976 Report of the Select Committee of the Economy, New York State Legislative Document No. 12, 1974.

Bendick, Marc, Jr., "Designing Circuit-Breaker Property Tax Relief," *National Tax Journal,* Vol. XXVII, No. 1, 1976, pp. 19-28.

Bergin, Thomas P., and William F. Eagen, "Economic Growth and Community Facilities," *Municipal Finance,* Vol. 33, May 1961, pp. 146-50.

Birch, David L., "The Processes Causing Economic Change in Cities," U.S. Department of Commerce, unpublished, 1978.

Bird, Richard M., "Tax-Subsidy Policies for Regional Development," *National Tax Journal,* Vol. XIX, No. 2, 1966, pp. 113-124.

Bishop, John, "Vouchers for Creating Jobs, Education, and Training," SR 17, The Institute for Research on Poverty, Madison, Wisc., 1977.

Black, David E., "Property Tax Incidence: The Excise-Tax Effect and Assessment Practices," *National Tax Journal,* Vol. XXX, December 1977, pp. 429-434.

Booth, Douglas, "The Differential Impact of Manufacturing and Mercantile Activity in Local Government Expenditures and Revenues," *National Tax Journal,* Vol. 31, 1978, pp. 33-47.

Bradford, David F., and Harry H. Kelejian, "An Econometric Model of the Flight to the Suburbs," *Journal of Political Economy,* Vol. 81, No. 3, May/June 1973, pp. 566-589.

Bradford, David F., and Wallace E. Oates, "Suburban Exploitation of Central Cities and Governmental Structure," in Harold M. Hochman and George E. Peterson, eds., *Redistribution Through Public Choice,* Columbia University Press, New York, 1974, pp. 43-90.

Break, George F., "Property Taxation: A Reappraisal of Burden Distribution, Incidence and Equity and their Policy Implications," in Arthur D. Lynn, ed., *Property Taxation, Land Uses and Public Policy.* Madison, University of Wisconsin Press, 1975.

Bridges, Benjamin, "State and Local Inducments for Industry, Part I," *National Tax Journal,* Vol. XVIII, No. 1, 1965, pp. 1-14, and "Part II," Vol. XVIII, No. 2, 1965, pp. 175-192.

Brinner, Roger E., and Charles T. Clotfelter, "An Economic Appraisal of State Lotteries," *National Tax Journal,* Vol. XXVIII, No. 4, 1975, pp. 395-403.

Bryce, Herrington, ed., *Revitalizing the City,* Lexington Books, Lexington, Mass., 1979.

Burns, Leland S., and Wing Ning Pang, "Big Business in the Big City," *Urban Affairs Quarterly,* Vol. 12, No. 4, June 1977, pp. 533-544.

Burnes, Honorable John W., "Federal Action to Strengthen State and Local Revenue Capabilities," *National Tax Journal,* Vol. XIV, No. 3, 1971, pp. 363-368.

Cahoon, C.R., and William R. Brown, "The Interstate Tax Dilemma-A Proposed Solution," *National Tax Journal,* Vol. 26, No. 2, 1973, pp. 187-197.

Cameron, Helen A., "Property Taxation as a Location Factor," *Bulletin of Business Research,* Vol. 44, 1969.

Campbell, Alan K., et al., *Urban Options I*, Academy for Contemporary Problems, Columbus, Ohio 1976.

Carlson, Gary E., "Property Taxes: The Implications for Cities: A Case for Land Value Taxation," *Commentary*, August 1977, pp. 12-13.

Cassidy, M.J., "Is a Progressive Tax Stabilizing?" *National Tax Journal*, Vol. XXIII, No. 2, 1970, pp. 194-205.

Cebula, R.J., "The Migration Impact of State and Local Government Policies: A Survey of the Literature in the United States." unpublished.

_____, "An Analysis of Migration Patterns and Local Government Policy Toward Public Education," *Public Choice*, Vol. 33, 1977, pp. 113-121.

_____, "A Note on Nonwhite Migration, Welfare Levels, and the Political Process," *Public Choice*, Vol. 28, 1976, pp. 117-119.

_____, "Interstate Migration and the Tiebout Hypothesis: An Analysis According to Race, Sex, and Age," *Journal of the American Statistical Association*, Vol. 69, 1974a, pp. 876-879.

_____, "Local Government Policies and Migration: An Analysis for SMSAs in the United States, 1965-1970." *Public Choice*, Vol. 19, 1974b, pp. 86-93.

_____, "The Quality of LIfe and Migration of the Elderly," *Review of Regional Studies*, Vol. 4, 1974c, pp. 62-68.

Chinitz, Benjamin, and Raymond Vernon, "Changing Forces in Industrial Relocation," *Harvard Business Review*, January 1960.

Coen, Robert M., and Brian J. Powell, "Theory and Measurement of the Incidence of Differential Property Taxes on Rental Housing," *National Tax Journal*, Vol. 25, June 1972, pp. 211-216.

Congressional Budget Office, *An Analysis of the Roth-Kemp Tax Cut Proposal*, Congress of the United States, Washington, D.C., October 1978.

Congressional Budget Office, *Proposition 13: Its Impact on the Nation's Economy, Federal Revenues, and Federal Expenditures*, Congress of the United States, Washington, D.c., July 1978.

CONSAD Research Corporation, *A Study of the Effects of Public Investment*, prepared for the Economic Development Administration, U.S. Department of Commerce, Washington, D.C., 1969.

Cook, Billy D., "The Circuit Breaker Approach for Granting Property Tax Relief," in ACIR, *Financing Schools and Property Tax Relief—A State Responsibility*, A-40, Washington, D.c., January 1973.

Cornia, Gary C., William A. Testa, and Frederick D. Stocker, *Local Fiscal Incentives and Economic Development*, Academy for Contemporary Problems, Dayton, Ohio, 1978.

Cuddington, John T., "Estimating the Impacts of Property Tax Reform," *Land Economics,* Vol. 54, No. 3, 1978, pp. 362-372.

Daicoff, Darwin W., "Capitalization of the Property Tax," Ph.D. dissertation, University of Michigan, 1961.

District of Columbia Tax Revision Commission, *Financing an Urban Government,* 1978.

Dorf, Ronald J., and M. Jarvin Emerson, "Determinants of Manufacturing Plant Location for Nonmetropolitan Communities in the West North Central Region of the U.S.," *Journal of Regional Science,* Vol. 18, No. 1, 1978, pp. 109-120.

Due, John F., "Studies of State-Local Tax Influences on Location of Industry," *National Tax Journal,* Vol. XIV, No. 2, 1961, pp. 163-173.

Ebel, Robert D., "Research and Policy Developments: Major Types of State and Local Taxes," in Municipal Finance Officers Association, *State and Local Government Finance and Financial Management: A Compendium of Current Research,* Washington, D.C., 1978.

Economic Development Administration, *Survey of Industrial Location Determinants,* U.S. Department of Commerce, Washington, D.C., 1971.

Edel, Matthew, and Elliot Sclar, "Taxes, Spending, and Property Values: Supply Adjustment in a Tiebout-Oates Model," *Journal of Political Economy,* Vol. 82, No. 5, 1974, pp. 941-954.

Ehrenberg, Ronald C., and Ronald L. Oaxaca, "Unemployment Insurance, Duration of Unemployment and Subsequent Wage Gain," *American Economic Review,* December, 1976, pp. 754-766.

Ellickson, Bryan, *Econometric Analysis of Urban Housing Markets: A New Approach,* The Rand Corporation, R-2024-NSF, July 1976.

Falk, Lawrence H., et al., *An Industrial Inducement Program for New Jersey,* Rutgers University, Bureau of Economic Research, no date.

Fantus Company, Inc., *The Appalachian Location Research Studies Program: Summary Report and Recommendations,* New York, 1976.

Feldstein, Martin S., "Temporary Layoffs in the Theory of Unemployment," *Journal of Political Economy,* Vol. 84, No. 5, 1976, pp. 937-958.

Fields, G.S., "Labor Force Migration, Unemployment and Job Turnover, *Review of Economics and Statistics,* Vol. 58, 1976, pp. 407-415.

Finkelstein, Philip, *Real Property Taxation in New York City,* New York, Praeger, 1975.

Fischel, William A., "An Evaluation of Proposals for Metropolitan Sharing of Commercial and Industrial Property Tax Base," *Journal of Urban Economics,* Vol. 3, 1976, pp. 253-263.

Fortune, Peter, "Financing P.L. 92-500: The Impact of the Federal Water Pollution Control Act of 1972 on the Municipal Bond Market," Report for the National Commission on Water Quality, Data Resources, Inc., September, 1975.

Fortune, Peter, "The Impact of Taxable Municipal Bonds: Policy Simulations with a Large Econometric Model," *National Tax Journal,* Vol. XXVI, No. 1, 1973, pp. 29-42.

Friedman, Joseph, *Housing Location and the Supply of Local Public Services,* P-5421, The Rand Corporation, April 1975.

Fuchs, Diane "State and Local Tax and Expenditure Limitations," Report for the Tax Reform Research Group, Washington, D.C., June 1978.

Fuchs, Victor R., *Changes in the Location of Manufacturing in the United States Since 1929,* Yale University Press, New Haven, 1962.

Fuller, Stephen S., and Joan E. Towles, "Impact of Intraurban Tax Differentials on Business and Residential Location in the Washington Metropolitan Area," prepared for the D.C. Tax Revision Commission, 1978.

Fulton, Maurice, "New Factors in Plant Location," *Harvard Business Review,* Vol. 49, 1971, pp. 4-17.

Gaffney, Mason, ed., *Extractive Resources and Taxation,* Madison: University of Wisconsin Press, 1967.

Gambling in America, Final Report of the Commission on the Review of the National Policy Toward Gambling, Washington, D.C., 1977.

Gerard, Karen, "New York City's Industrial Tax Structure," unpublished paper, Chase Manhattan Bank, New York, 1974.

Gerweck, John E., and Donald J. Epp, "The Effect of Industrial Growth on the Local Real Estate Tax: an Expanded Model," *Land Economics,* Vol. 50, No. 4, 1974, pp. 397-401.

Goldfarb, Robert S., and Anthony M.J. Yezer, "Evaluating Alternative Theories of Intercity and Interregional Wage Differentials," *Journal of Regional Science,* Vol. 16, No. 3, 1976, pp. 345-363.

Greene, Kenneth V., William G. Neenan, and Claudia D. Scott, "Fiscal Incidence in the Washington Metropolitan Area," *Land Economics,* Vol. 52, No. 1, February 1976, pp. 13-31.

Greenwood, Michael J., "Research on Internal Migration in the United States: A Survey," *Journal of Economic Literature,* Vol. 13, June 1975, pp. 397-433.

Greytak, David, and Bernard Jump, *The Effects of Inflation on State and Local Government Finances, 1967-74,* Occasional Paper No. 25, Syracuse, New York, 1975.

Greytak, David, and Edward N. Cupoli, "Changes in Central City Employment, Resident Decentralization, and Personal Income Tax Revenues," paper presented
149

to the Meetings of the Northeast Regional Science Association, Summer 1977.

Grieson, Ronald E., et al., "The Effect of Business Taxation on the Location of Industry," *Journal of Urban Economics*, Vol. 4, 1977, pp. 170-185.

Groves, Harold, and John Riew, "The Impact of Industry on Local Taxes—A Sample Model," *National Tax Journal*, Vol. XVI, No. 2, 1963, pp. 137-146.

Grubb, W. Norton, and E. Gareth Hoachlander, "Circuit Breaker Schedules and Their Application to California," *Policy Analysis*, 1978, pp. 317-337.

Gurwitz, Aaron, "The Economic Effects of Property Tax Abatement for Industry," unpublished paper, Department of Economics, Michigan State University, 1977.

Halstead, D. Kent, *The Tax Wealth of Fifty States*, National Institute for Education, Washington, D.C., 1978.

Hamilton, Bruce W., *Property Taxes and the Tiebout Hypothesis: Some Empirical Evidence*, Working Paper 1204-23, The Urban Institute, Washington, D.C., February 1972.

Hamilton, Edward K., and Francine Rabinovitz, "Federalization of Welfare: The Financial Effects," in George Peterson (ed.), *Fiscal Choices*, The Urban Institute, Washington, D.C., forthcoming.

Hamovitch, William, "Effects of Increases in Sales Tax Rates on Taxable Sales in New York City," *Financing Government in New York City*, Graduate School of Public Administration of New York University Report to the Temporary Commission on City Finances, New York University, 1966.

Hanna, Frank A., *State Income Differentials*, Duke University Press, Durham, North Carolina, 1959.

Harris, Curtis C., and Frank E. Hopkins, *Locational Analysis*, Lexington Books, Lexington, Massachusetts, 1972.

Harrison, Bennett, "The Political Economy of State Job Creation Business Incentives," *Journal of the American Institute of Planners*, November 1978.

_____, *The Economic Development of Massachusetts*, prepared for the Joint Committee on Commerce and Labor of the Massachusetts State Legislature, November 1974.

_____, *Urban Economic Development*, The Urban League, Washington, D.C., 1974.

_____, and Sandra Kanter, "The Great State Robbery," *Working Papers for a New Society*, Spring 1976, pp. 54-66.

Harriss, C. Lowell, "Property Taxation After the California Vote," *Tax Review*, The Tax Foundation, August 1978.

Hartnett, Harry D., "Industrial Climate in Central Cities," *American Industrial Development Conference Journal*, Vol. 7, No. 2, April 1972, pp. 19-38.

Haskins, Gage B.A., "The Impact of International Trade and Investment Policy on Employment in the United States: A Policy Briefing Paper," prepared for the Department of Housing and Urban Development, November 1977, mimeographed.

Heinberg, John D., and Wallace E. Oates, "The Incidence of Differential Property Taxes on Rental Housing: an Addendum," *National Tax Journal*, Vol. 25, June 1972, pp. 221-222.

_____, The Incidence of Differential Property Taxes on Rental Housing: A Comment and Further Evidence," *National Tax Journal*, Vol. 23, March 1970, pp. 92-98.

Hellerstein, Jerome R., "State Tax Discrimination Against Out-of-Staters," *National Tax Journal*, Vol. XXX, No. 2, June 1977, pp. 113-134.

_____, "Multinational Corporations and Income Allocation Under Section 482 of the Internal Revenue Code," *Harvard Law Review*, Vol. 89, 1976, pp. 1202-38.

_____, "The Unitary Business Principle and Multicorporate Enterprises: An Examination of the Major Controversies," *The Tax Executive*, July 1975.

Hellman, Daryl A., and Costas Sifniotis, "Distributional Considerations of Property Tax Exemption: Analytical Framework," *Public Finance Quarterly*, January 1977, pp. 127-135.

Hellman, Daryl, Gregory H. Wassall, and Herb Escowitz, "The Role of Statewide Industrial Incentive Programs in the New England Economy," *New England Journal of Business and Economy*, Vol. 1, 1973, pp. 10-29.

Hellman, Daryl A., Gregory H. Wassall, and Lawrence H. Falk, *State Financial Incentives to Industry*, Lexington Books, Lexington, Mass., 1976.

Hodge, James H., "A Study of Regional Investment Decisions," Ph.D. dissertation, University of Chicago, March, 1979.

Hogan, Timothy D., and Robert B. Shelton, "Interstate Tax Exportation and States' Fiscal Structures," *National Tax Journal*, Vol. 26, No. 4, 1973, pp. 77-84.

Holcombe, Randall C., "The Florida System: A Bowen Equilibrium Referendum Process," *National Tax Journal*, Vol. 30, No. 1, March 1977, pp. 77-84.

Hyman, David N., and E.C., Pasour, "Real Property Taxes, Local Public Services, and Residential Property Values," *Southern Economic Journal*, Vol. 39, No. 4, April 1973, pp. 601-611.

Izraeli, Oded, "Differences in National Income and Prices Between Cities," Ph.D. dissertation, University of Chicago, 1973.

Jack Fawcett Associates, Inc., *Effectiveness of Financial Incentives on Investment in the Economic Development Administration's Designated Areas*, Economic Development Administration, Washington, D.C., 1976.

James, Franklin, "Income Taxes, Homeownership, and Urban Land Use," Paper presented at the American Economic Association meetings, New Jersey, 1976.

Jones, H.C., Mike et al., *An Analysis of the 1973-74 Energy Shortage in the New York Region,* BNL 20133, Brookhaven National Laboratory, New York, 1975.

Jusenius, Carol L., and L.L. Ledebur, *Documenting the Decline of the North,* Economic Development Administration, Washington, D.C., June 1978.

_____, *A Myth in the Making: The Southern Economic Challenge and Northern Economic Decline,* Economic Development Administration, November, 1976.

_____, *Firms in New England: Deaths, Births and Migration,* forthcoming.

Kee, Woo Sik, "Industrial Development and Its Impact on Local Finance," *Quarterly Review of Economics and Statistics,* April, 1968, pp. 19-24.

Kemper, Peter, *Manufacturing Location, Production Requirements, and Market Characteristics,* Unpublished, 1974.

Laidler, David, "Income Tax Incentives for Owner-Occupied Housing," in A.C. Harberger and M.J. Bailey, eds., *The Taxation of Income from Capital,* The Brookings Institution, Washington, D.C., 1969.

Ledebur, Larry, "Regional Location and Performance of Manufacturing in the United States," unpublished, The Urban Institute, October, 1978.

Levin, Sharon C., "Suburban-Central City Property Tax Differentials and the Location of Industry: Some Evidence," *Land Economics,* Vol. 50, No. 4, November, 1974, pp. 380-386.

Levy, Mickey, "Voting on California's Tax and Expenditure Limitation Initiative," *National Tax Journal,* Vol. 28, No. 4, 1975, pp. 426-435.

Lile, Stephen E., and Don M. Soule, "Interstate Differences in Family Tax Burdens," *National Tax Journal,* Vol. 22, No. 4, 1969, pp. 433-445.

Lindholm, Richard M., ed., *Property Tax Reform: Foreign and United States Experience with Site Value Taxation,* Monograph 77-11, Lincoln Institute of Land Policy, Cambridge, Mass., 1977.

Liu, B.C., "Local Government Finance and Metropolitan Employment Growth: A Simultaneous Equation Model," *Southern Economic Journal,* Vol. 43, 1977, pp. 1379-1385.

Loewenstein, Louis K., "The New York Urban Development Corporation—A Forgotten Failure or a Precursor of the Future?" *Journal of the American Institute of Planners,* July 1978, pp. 261-273.

Lynn, Arthur D., Jr., "Legal and Public Policy Aspects of Implementing Site Value Taxation," in Lindholm, ed., *Property Tax Reform.*

Manvel, Allen D., "Differences in Fiscal Capcity and Effort: Their Significance for a Federal Revenue Sharing System," *National Tax Journal,* Vol. 24, No. 2, 1971, pp. 193-204.

152 Maxwell, James A., and J. Robert Aronson, *Financing State and Local Government,*

The Brookings Institution, Washington, D.C., 1977.

Mayo, Stephen K., "Local Public Goods and Residential Location: An Empirical Test of the Tiebout Hypothesis," paper presented to the Metropolitan Governance Committee, Resources for the Future, Washington, D.C. 1973.

_____ , "An Econometric Model of Residential Location," Ph.D. Dissertation, Harvard University, Cambridge, Mass., 1971.

McClure, Charles E., "The New View of the Property Tax: A Caveat," *National Tax Journal*, Vol. 30, No. 1, 1977, pp. 69-76.

Mieszkowski, Peter, "The Property Tax: An Excise Tax or a Profit Tax?" *Journal of Public Economics*, Vol. 1, April 1972, pp. 73-96.

Mikesell, John L., "Central Cities and Sales Tax Rate Differentials: The Border City Problem," *National Tax Journal*, Vol. 23, No. 2, 1970, pp. 206-213.

Miller, Stephen M., and William K. Tabb, "A New Look at a Pure Theory of Local Expenditures," *National Tax Journal*, Vol. 26, 1973, pp. 161-176.

Moes, Joe E., "The Subsidization of Industry by Local Communities in the South," *Southern Economic Journal*, Vol. 28, October 1961.

Moody, James, "Measuring Tax Benefit and Capitalization from a Local Rapid Transit Investment in the San Francisco Bay Area," Ph.D. dissertation, University of California at Berkeley, 1974.

Morgan, William E., *Taxes and the Location of Industry*, University of Colorado Press, Boulder, 1967.

Morgan, William E., and Merlin M. Hackbart, "An Analysis of State and Local Industrial Tax Exemption Programs," *Southern Economic Journal*, Vol. 41, No. 2, 1976, pp. 200-205.

Moscovitch, Edward, "State Graduated Income Taxes—A State Initiated Form of Federal Revenue Sharing," *National Tax Journal*, Vol. 25, 1972, pp. 53-64.

Moses, Leon, and M.F. Williamson, "The Location of Economic Activity in Cities," *American Economic Review*, Vol. 57, 1967.

Morris, Frank, "The Taxable Bond Option," *National Tax Journal*, Vol. 29, No. 3, 1976.

Mulkey, David, and B.L. Dillman, "Location and the Effects of State and Local Development Subsidies," *Growth and Change*, Vol. 7, April 1976, pp. 71-80.

Municipal Finance Officers Association, *State and Local Government Finance and Financial Management: Compendium of Current Research*, Washington, D.C., August 1978.

National Governors' Association, *Allocation of State Funds for Jurisdictions*, Washington, D.C., 1978a.

_____, *Tax and Expenditure Limitations 1978,* Washington, D.C., 1978b.

_____, *Targeting of Federal and State Aid to Distressed Cities,* Washington, D.C., forthcoming.

National League of Cities, *The Tax System: Consequences for Urban Policy,* Washington, D.C., 1977.

Netzer, Dick, "The Incidence of the Property Tax Revisited," *National Tax Journal,* Vol. 26, No. 4, 1973, pp. 515-535.

Neufield, John, "Tax Rate Referenda and the Property Taxpayers' Revolt," *National Tax Journal,* Vol. 30, No. 4, 1977, pp. 441-456.

Oates, Wallace E., "The Effects of Property Taxes and Local Public Services on Property Values: An Empirical Study of Tax Capitalization and the Tiebout Hypothesis," *Journal of Political Economy,* Vol. 77, Nov/Dec. 1969, pp. 957-971.

Oldman, Oliver, and Mary Miles Teachout, "Land Valuation Under a Separate Tax on Land," Proceedings of the 70th Annual Conference on Taxation, National Tax Association, Chicago, 1977.

Olvey, L.D., "Regional Growth and Interregional Migration—Their Patterns of Interaction," *Review of Regional Studies,* Vol. 2, No. 2, 1972, pp. 139-163.

Orr, Larry L., "The Incidence of Differential Property Taxes on Urban Housing: Reply," *National Tax Journal,* Vol. 25, No. 2, 1972, pp. 217-220.

_____, "The Incidence of Differential Property Taxes on Urban Housing," *National Tax Journal,* Vol. 21, No. 3, 1968, pp. 253-262.

Ostrovsky, A., "Some Economic Effects and Causes of State and Local Government Commitment to Public Education," *Indian Journal of Economics,* Vol. 60, 1978, pp. 49-58.

Pack, Howard, and Janet Rothenberg Pack, "Metropolitan Fragmentation and Suburban Homogeneity," *Urban Studies,* Vol. 14, 1977, pp. 191-201.

Pack, Janet Rothenberg, "Determinants of Migration to Central Cities," *Journal of Regional Science,* vol. 13, 1973, pp. 249-260.

Pechman, Joseph A. *Federal Tax Policy,* The Brookings Institution, Washington, D.C. 1966.

Pechman, Joseph A., and Benjamin Okner, *Who Bears the Tax Burden,* The Brookings Institution, Washington, D.C., 1974.

Perloff, Harvey S., et al., *How a Region Grows,* Committee for Economic Development, Supplementary Paper No. 17, Washington, D.C., March 1973.

Peterson, George E., "Differential Taxation of Land and Improvements," report prepared for the D.C. Tax Revision Commission, Washington D.C., 1978a.

_____, *Federal Tax Policy and Urban Development,* The Urban Institute,

Washington, D.C., 1978b.

_____, "Finance," in William Gorman and William Glazer, eds., *The Urban Predicament,* The Urban Institute, Washington, D.C., 1976.

_____, Testimony Before the Committee on Banking, Currency and Housing, U.S. House of Representatives, Washington, D.C., September 28, 1976.

_____, and Harvey Galper, "Tax Exempt Financing of Private Industry's Pollution Control Investment," *Public Policy,* Vol. 23, 1975, pp. 81-103.

_____, et al., *Property Taxes and Housing in Central Cities,* D.C. Heath and Co., Lexington, Mass., 1973.

Pfister, R.L., "A Re-evaluation of the Justifications for Property Tax Exemptions," *Public Finance Quarterly,* October, 1976, pp. 431-452.

Polinsky, A. Mitchell, and Daniel L. Rubinfeld, "The Long Run Effects of a Residential Property Tax," *Journal of Urban Economics,* Vol. 5, April, 1978, pp. 241-262.

Pollack, W., "Pricing Fire Protection Services," in Selma Mushkin, ed., *Public Prices for Public Goods,* The Urban Institute, Washington, 1972.

Pollock, Richard L., and Daniel C. Shoup, "The Effect of Shifting the Property Tax from Improvements to Land Values: An Empirical Estimate," *Land Economics,* Vol. 67, 1977.

Rafuse, Robert W., "The New York State Personal Income Tax: Essays in Fiscal Analysis," prepared for the New York State Temporary State Commission on State and Local Finances, December, 1974.

Renas, S.M., and R. Kumar, "The Cost of Living, Labor Market Opportunities, and the Decision to Migrate: A Case of Misspecification," *Annals of Regional Science,* Vol. 12, 1978, pp. 65-74.

Rinehart, J., "Rates of Return on Municipal Subsidies to Industry," *Southern Economic Journal,* April 1963.

Roniger, George, *Testimony before the Committee on Taxation and Government Operations,* New York State Senate, 1/26/78.

Ross, D. William, "Tax Exemption in Louisiana as a Device for Encouraging Industrial Development," *Southwestern Social Science Quarterly,* June 1953, pp. 14-22.

Sahlings, Leonard, "Are State and City Corporate Income Taxes Stifling Investment in New York City?" *Federal Reserve Bank of New York,* December 1978.

Samaza, Gerald W., "A Benefit Cost Analysis of a Regional Development Incentive: State Loans," *Journal of Regional Science,* Vol. 10, 1970.

Schaefer, Jeffrey M., "Sales Tax Regressivity Under Alternative Tax Bases and Income Concepts," *National Tax Journal,* Vol. 22, No. 4, 1969, pp. 516-527.

Schmenner, Roger, "City Taxes and Industrial Location," unpublished paper, Harvard, 1974.

Shannon, John, "After Jarvis—Hard Questions for State-Local Policymakers," Testimony before the Subcommittee on Intergovernmental Relations of the Senate Committee on Government Affairs, June 28, 1978.

_____, "Property Taxation: Federalism and Federal Policy," in Arthur D. Lynn, Jr., ed., *Property Taxation, Land Use and Public Policy,* University of Wisconsin Press, 1976a.

_____, Testimony before the House Committee on Banking, Currency and Housing, reprinted by the Committee as *The Rebirth of the American City,* Part 2, U.S. House of Representatives, Washington, D.C., 1976b, p. 807ff.

_____, "The Property Tax: Reform or Relief?" in George E. Peterson, ed., Property Tax Reform, The Urban Institute, Washington, D.C., 1973.

_____, "Federal Assistance in Modernizing State Sales and Local Property Taxes," *National Tax Journal,* Vol. 24, No. 3, 1971, pp. 379-388.

_____, "Federal Assistance in Modernizing State Sales and Local Property Taxes," *National Tax Journal,* Vol. 29, No. 3, 1976c, pp. 379-388.

_____, and Carol S. Weissert, "After Jarvis: Tough Questions for Fiscal Policy-makers," *Intergovernmental Perspective,* Vol. 4, No. 3, 1978.

Shaul, Marnie, *The Taxable Bond Option for Municipal Bonds,* Academy for Contemporary Problems, Columbus, Ohio, October, 1977.

Sherman, Roger, and Thomas D. Willett, "Regional Development Externalities, and Tax-Subsidy Combinations," *National Tax Journal,* Vol. 22, No. 2, 1969, pp. 291-300.

Smith, David Mitchell, "Neoclassical Growth Models and Regional Growth in the U.S., *Journal of Regional Science,* Vol. 15, No. 2, 1975.

Smith, V. Kerry, and Timothy A. Keyak, "A Comparison of Tax Capitalization Effects on Owner Occupied and Rental Housing in the United States," *Applied Economics,* Vol. 7, 1975, pp. 167-174.

Smith, R. Stafford, "Property Tax Capitalization in San Francisco," *National Tax Journal,* Vol. 23, No. 2, June 1970, pp. 177-193.

Stanfield, Rochelle L., "There are Surpluses in the Statehouses—But Can They Last Forever? *National Tax Journal,* 1/21/78, pp. 95-99.

Steinnes, Donald N., "Causality and Intraurban Location," *Journal of Urban Economics,* Vol. 4, No. 1, 1977, pp. 59-79.

Sternlieb, George, and Robert W. Burchell, *Residential Abandonment: The Tenement Landlord Revisited,* Center for Urban Policy Research, Rutgers, The State University of New Jersey, 1973.

Stinson, Thomas F., *State Taxation of Mineral Deposits and Production,* Interagency Energy Environment Research and Development of the USDA and EPA, Washington, D.C., 1977.

Stober, William J., and Lawrence H. Falk, "Industrial Development Bonds as a Subsidy to Industry," *National Tax Journal,* Vol. 22, No. 2, 1969, pp. 232-243.

_____, "Property Tax Exemptions: An Inefficient Subsidy to Industry," *National Tax Journal,* Vol. 20, No. 4, 1967.

Stockfish, J.A., *A Study of California's Tax Treatment of Manufacturing Industry,* California's Economic Development Agency, Sacramento, 1961.

Stolz, Otto C., and George A. Purdy, "Tax Simplification and Efficiency Through Federal Collection," report by the Advocates and Analysts, Arlington, Va., June, 1977.

Stone, Donald B., *Industrial Location in Metropolitan Areas,* Praeger, New York, 1976.

Struyk, Raymond J., "Spatial Concentration of Manufacturing Employment in Metropolitan Areas," *Economic Geography,* Vol. 48, No. 2, 1972, pp. 189-192.

_____and Franklin James, *Intermetropolitan Industrial Location: The Pattern and Process of Change in Four Metropolitan Areas,* Lexington Books, Lexington, Mass., 1975.

Suits, Daniel B., "Gambling Taxation in the District of Columbia," paper prepared for the D.C. Tax Revision Commission, Washington, D.C., 1978.

Surrey, Stanley S., "Tax Incentives as a Device for Implementing Government Policy: A Comparison with Direct Government Expenditures," *Harvard Law Review,* Vol. 83, No. 4, January 1970, pp. 705-738.

U.S. Department of Agriculture, *State Taxation of Mineral Deposits and Production,* Rural Development Research Report No. 2, Washington, D.C., 1978.

Vasquez, Thomas, and Charles deSeve, "State/Local Taxes and Jurisdictional Shifts in Corporate Business Activity: The Complications of Measurement," *National Tax Journal,* Vol. 30, No. 3, 1977, pp. 285-298.

Vaughan, Roger J., "Federal Policy and Local Fiscal Conditions," paper presented at HUD conference on the urban impacts of federal policies, Washington, D.C., February 1979.

_____, *The Urban Impacts of Federal Policies: Vol. 2 Economic Development,* The Rand Corporation, R-2028-KF/RC, July 1977.

_____and Mary E. Vogel, *The Urban Impacts of Federal Policies: Vol. 4, Population and Residential Location,* The Rand Corporation, R-2205-KF/HEW, March 1979.

Vernez, Georges, and Roger Vaughan, *Assessment of Countercyclical Public Works and Public Employment Programs,* The Rand Corporation, R-2214-EDA, *157*

September, 1978.

Vernez, Georges et al., *Regional Cycles and Employment Effects of Public Works Investments,* The Rand Corporation, R-2052-EDA, January 1977.

Wead, Jim, and Lois R. Koepf, *Coal: State Severance Taxes and the Distribution of Revenue,* Lexington, Kentucky, Council of State Governments, 1976.

Weicher, John W., "Determinants of Central City Expenditures: Some Overlooked Factors and Problems," *National Tax Journal,* Vol. 23, No. 4, 1970, pp. 379-396.

Weinstein, Bernard L., "Tax Incentives for Growth," *Society,* Vol. 14, No. 3, 1977, pp. 73-75.

_____, and Robert E. Firestines, *Regional Growth and Decline in the United States,* Praeger, New York, 1978.

Wheat, Leonard F., *Regional Growth and Industrial Location,* Lexington Books, Lexington, Mass., 1973.

White, Michelle J., and Lawrence J. White, "Tax Subsidy to Owner-Occupied Housing: Who Benefits?" *Journal of Public Economics,* Vol. 3, 1977, p. 111-126.

Williams, William V., et al., "The Stability, Growth, and Stabilizing Influence of State Taxes," *National Tax Journal,* Vol. 26, No. 2, 1973, pp. 267-273.

_____, "A Measure of the Impact of State and Local Taxes on Industry Location," *Journal of Regional Science,* Summer 1967, pp. 49-59.

Wisconsin Department of Revenue, *Corporate Tax Climate: A Comparison of 15 States,* Madison, Wisconsin, December 1975.

Wolman, Hal, "Components of Employment Change in Local Economies," Report 1264-02, The Urban Institute, Washington, D.C., 1978.

Zimmerman, Dennis, "Expenditure-Tax Incidence Studies, Public Higher Education, and Equity," *National Tax Journal,* Vol. 26, No. 1, 1973, pp. 65-70.

STUDIES IN STATE DEVELOPMENT POLICY

Please send me the following publications:

Quantity	Title	No.	Price	Total
_____	State Taxation and Economic Development	3614	$9.95	_____
_____	Economic Development: The Challenge of the 1980s	3610	$9.95	_____
_____	Innovations in Development Finance	3612	$9.95	_____
_____	Labor Market Segmentation	3611	$8.95	_____
_____	Inflation and Unemployment	3618	$8.95	_____
_____	Democratizing the Development Process	3616	$7.95	_____
_____	Job Creation	3613	$8.95	_____
_____	Impact Assessment	3617	$8.95	_____
_____	The Capital Budget	3615	$8.95	_____
	TOTAL ORDER			_____

☐ Payment enclosed (no charge for handling and postage)

☐ Please bill me (postage and $2 handling charge will be added)

Payment must accompany all orders under $20.

Name: _____

Title: _____

Address: _____

_____

City, State, Zip _____

Make checks payable to the Council of State Planning Agencies.

Important Note: Discounts of 10% are available on any order of four or more titles. A discount of 20% is available to individuals and institutions ordering the entire nine-volume series ($60.00 per set). Full payment must accompany requests for discounts.